WORLD SECURITY
for the
21ST CENTURY:

Challenges and Solutions

A Colloquium Between American and Soviet Legal Experts

BENJAMIN B. FERENCZ, Editor

Sponsored by

The Pace Peace Center, Pace Law School, White Plains, New York

ISBN 0-379-20466-5

THE CHALLENGE

We have in this past year made great progress in ending the long era of conflict and cold war. We have before us the opportunity to forge for ourselves and for future generations a new world order, a world where the rule of law, not the law of the jungle, governs the conduct of nations. **U.S President George Bush, Address to the Nation, January 16, 1991.**

This is a new and different world. . . It is in our hands. . . to cap a historic movement towards a new world order and a long era of peace...We have a vision of a new partnership of nations that transcends the Cold War. . .We must join together in a new compact --all of us --to bring the United Nations into the 21st century. . . Let it be said of the final decade of the 20th Century: This was a time when humankind came into its own. **U.S. President Bush, Address to the U.N. General Assembly, Oct. 1, 1990.**

The crisis in the Persian Gulf, as grave as it is, also offers a rare opportunity to move toward an historic period of cooperation. . . a new world order can emerge: a new era, freer from the threat of terror, stronger in the pursuit of justice, and more secure in the quest for peace. **U.S. President Bush, Address to Joint Session of Congress, Sept. 11, 1990.**

To prevent anarchy. . . I know of nothing but the rule of law. No one , no State, no philosophy has a monopoly on law. . . We all know that there can be lasting peace and freedom in relationships between peoples only if States agree to follow common rules. . .The time has come for international law to reign. . We are faced with a choice between the law of the jungle and the rule of law. **French President Mitterand, Address to the U.N. General Assembly, 27 Sept. 1990.**

Iraq has committed an unprovoked act of aggression...An act which one can unquestionably describe without exaggeration as an act of terrorism has been perpetrated against the emerging new world order. This is a major affront to mankind. Unless we find a way to respond to it and deal with the situation, civilization will be set back half a century. **USSR Foreign Minister Shevardnadze, Address to the UN General Assembly, 25 Sept. 1990.**

The united Germany...shall help Europe meet its responsibility in shaping the emerging new world order... A new concept of the coexistence of nations is taking shape. It is based on the awareness of the global challenges and of global interdependence... The opportunity for developing a new world order lies in solidarity and joint action. The settlement of conflicts by military means is becoming increasingly outlawed. Rule of law is acquiring greater significance...The task of the United Nations in this decade is to develop the international legal system further in order to ensure mankind's survival. **German Foreign Minister Genscher, Address to the UN General Assembly, 26 Sept. 1990.**

If the United States and the other nations that have pledged to boycott Hussein hold fast, we will not just win a war but we will have created a new world order, one in which armed aggression is not tolerated. In the new world that we have an opportunity to create, law will govern and it will be enforced by economic power. **U.S. Businessman Howard S. Brembeck, President of Fourth Freedom Forum, Goshen, Indiana; author of** ***The Civilized Defense Plan (1990).***

The United States should capitalize on the new enlightenment at work in the world by dedicating itself to taking the lead in bringing into being an effective world security arrangement, a world governed by law. **Jack Kidd, Major General, U.S. Air Force (Ret.); Author of** ***The Strategic Cooperation Initiative*** **(1988).**

HOW DO WE CREATE THE NEW WORLD ORDER CALLED FOR BY THE WORLD'S LEADERS? THAT IS THE CHALLENGE ADDRESSED BY THE COLLOQUIUM HERE RECORDED.

This book is respectfully dedicated to those of every nationality or persuasion who long for a new world order in which all may live in peace and dignity.

PACE UNIVERSITY SCHOOL OF LAW
Pace Peace Center
Conference Agenda

On behalf of the Pace Peace Center, I am pleased to extend a very cordial welcome to our friends from the Soviet Union! We hope your stay in the United States will be pleasant and will serve the cause of world peace.

Our objective is to begin a process whereby international lawyers, free of political ties, can help to construct the legal framework for a more rational global society where the force of law will replace the law of force.

A provisional agenda is attached. You will note that it focuses on three fundamental structures which are essential for every orderly society:

1. Laws—to define minimum standards of international conduct;

2. Courts—to determine if the laws have been violated and to serve as a forum for the peaceful adjudication of disputes; and

3. Enforcement—which requires some managing agency, control of arms, effective sanctions or an international force and enhanced social justice.

These are broad outlines only. Thus, under the heading of "Courts" one would have to consider all other means for peaceful resolution of conflict, such as mediation, arbitration, conciliation, negotiation etc. One would also consider an International Criminal Court as well as courts like Human Rights Courts and the Law of the Sea Tribunal. These can be considered during the discussion under each heading. All constructive ideas are welcome.

The United Nations has declared this "The Decade of International Law" Let us make that goal a reality for the betterment and tranquility of all humankind.

Sincerely,
Benjamin B. Ferencz
Executive Director

TABLE OF CONTENTS

INTRODUCTION by Professor Benjamin B. Ferencz i
PREFACE by Professor Louis B. Sohn iii
List of Participants and Organizations v

I. WORLD SECURITY FOR THE 21ST CENTURY

Introductory Dialogue: International Law and Order 1
Reevaluating Existing Legal Mechanisms 9
Problems Posed by State Sovereignty 18
Improving the United Nations Charter 23
Changing International Law to Meet Changing Times 33
Enforcing International Law: UN Peacekeeping 39
The Draft Code of Crimes Against Peace and Security 43
    New International Crimes 44
    An International Criminal Court 47
Improving the International Court of Justice 53
    Other International Courts 61
Dispute Settlement by Negotiation 63
Improving the UN General Assembly 71
Arms Control 79
    Verification: Problems and Solutions 79
    Arms Census and "Transparency" 83
    Additional Means of Making Arms Control Effective 86
    Defensive Defense 89
    The McCloy-Zorin Agreement on Universal Disarmament 93
The Enhanced Role of the Indiividual in International Law 95
International Law and World Environmental Problems 103
Visions of a World Federation of Peace and Justice: 111
    The Coming European "Home" 117
Revisiting the International Court of Justice 119
An Evolutionary View of World Needs 125

II. CONFERENCE REVIEW HELD AT UNITED NATIONS
HEADQUARTERS 133

Outline of Prior Discussions 133
Internal Critique 135
Need for a Comprehensive System 139
Disarmament as Seen from the United Nations 144

III. MEETING RESUMED AT PLEASANTVILLE WITH UKRAINIAN
DELEGATION 153

A Brief Review 154
The Right to a Healthy Environment 159
Creating an International Legal Order 161
Generating Political Will 173
Enhancing Dispute Settlement by Peaceful Means 179
Managing the Planet More Efficiently 187
Social Justice and Peace 192
Dealing with Outlaw Nations: The Problem of Sanctions 199

IV. BIBLIOGRAPHY OF LAW BOOKS ON PEACE 203

INTRODUCTION

The world is in ferment and the old order must yield to the new. The system of international security in the 21st century will no longer resemble the policies of the past. The emergence of a new cooperative spirit between the Soviet Union and the United States holds great promise for the future. In building that future on a firm foundation, lawyers will have to play an important role.

Acting on behalf of the Pace Peace Center, I invited a number of distinguished Soviet legal experts to come to the United States for a week at the Pace campus at Pleasantville, New York in order to discuss the future world order with informed international lawyers from the United States and the United Nations. The discussions were frank, informal and informative. They covered the entire range of problems that will have to be addressed and resolved if the rule of law is to replace the law of force.

The number of participants varied with each session. In all, there were no more than fifteen. We sat around a small table and exchanged views on the vital problems of our times. The recorded transcript of those conversations - edited only as necessary for clarity and to avoid repetition - is attached. It is, I believe, a unique dialogue between dreamers and realists striving together to create the foundations for a more tranquil and just international society. Such deliberations will be essential for all those who seek to build the new world order of the future.

Appreciation is expressed to Sandra Bendfeldt who made the initial contacts with some of the Soviet guests. Dr. Rose Cooper arranged dormitory accommodations and facilities. My wife, Gertrude, was generally helpful, as was Richard Duffee. Without their help, the conference would not have been possible. U.N. Senior Legal Officer, Roy S. Lee arranged the meeting room at the U.N. Philip Cohen, Publisher of Oceana Publications provided the recording machines. His Senior Editor, Susan De Maio managed the printing, and Nicholas Brandi helped solve computer problems. I thank them all for their important contributions.

We hope we have begun a process which will serve the interests of peace and humanity.

Benjamin B. Ferencz
Executive Director, Pace Peace Center
Senior Special Fellow, United Nations Institute for Training and Research (UNITAR)
December 1, 1990
New Rochelle, New York

PREFACE

Since the days of Socrates and Plato problems have been successfully analyzed through dialogues. It is not surprising, therefore, that Ben Ferencz, a prolific writer, a dissector of mankind's troubles, and, last but not least, a professor of international law especially interested in the study of international institutions, has decided to start a dialogue with Soviet experts on the future of global security. This book, **World Security for the 21st Century: Challenges and Solutions**, is a transcript of that dialogue. Participants included Soviet researchers in such fields as arms control, environment, international law and international courts, and their American counterparts, as well as some experts from the United Nations staff and several non-governmental organizations.

After the initial hesitations were dispelled, the discussion livened, and the participants started moving rapidly from topic to topic, pointing out the links between various problems and the need to solve them simultaneously. Sovereignty cannot be abolished, but certain tasks can be entrusted to common international institutions. International courts are viewed by governments with a large amount of suspicion, but this is mostly due to the fact that there are only few cases presented to them, often rather hopeless cases, sent to a court only after countries have struggled with them for a long time without success. No wonder that an international court cannot solve such problems to the satisfaction of all the parties. Nevertheless, amazingly most court decisions are accepted by the parties, sometimes grudgingly but more often with a sigh of relief that the subject is closed and they can proceed to other problems on their agenda.

The participants struggled also with such new concepts as the participation of individuals in the international legal order. International standards of behavior must be observed not only by states, but also by various organizations, by transnational corporations and above all by individuals. It is too often forgotten that states, organizations or corporations do not make the decisions on which the future of mankind depends; they are made by individuals—kings, presidents, prime ministers, and directors of corporations, large and small, and by concurrent pressure of millions of individuals expressing their opinions on global problems, sometimes by their ballots but more often by their activities in the political, economic, social and even cultural arenas. Reasonable orders by superior authorities are usually obeyed, but when rulers start abusing their powers or show their incompetence in controlling world-changing events, the will of the people manifests itself and the rulers discover that they are no longer molders of public opinion but the objects of its wrath. Old leaders are replaced, new leaders emerge and suddenly the situation changes drastically and a new order emerges in one country after another. Rights and duties of states are being replaced by rights and duties of individuals. The revolutions of the past were mostly revolutions within the states and usually affect only a few countries or only one area of the world. Today we are witnessing, however, development of popular movements for drastic changes all over the world.

It is amazing that these changes have been accomplished largely in a peaceful manner. There is danger, nevertheless that the old habits will not disappear completely. There is always a possibility that a nation will follow its ambitious leader into dangerous ventures, and may try to benefit from the fact that the rest of the world is preoccupied with other problems. Though war has been outlawed, aggressions and civil wars persist. The international community has to learn to deal firmly with the violators of the basic rules of international law, and the United Nations has to be permitted to use energetically the powers that were bestowed upon it in 1945. In all social orders there is strength in unity. Humanity has learned to unite in cities, principalities and finally states, and to maintain peace in areas embracing whole continents. The time has come to do it on the global scale. The golden age is not a period in the dim past, but is ahead of us.

The consensus necessary for us to reach a better future can best be built by patient and incisive discussions such as recorded in this book. We should be grateful to Professor Ferencz and his guests from two continents for starting this dialogue and showing us that reasonable people can be found throughout the world. Thinking together they multiply their strength and can bring about peace, freedom and prosperity for all mankind.

Louis B. Sohn
Woodruff Professor of International Law, University of Georgia School of Law
Athens, Georgia, U.S.A.
Bemis Professor of International Law, Emeritus, Harvard Law School.
President, American Society of International Law, 1988-1990.
31 October 1990

Conference on International Law and Peace for the 21st Century June 22—July 1, 1990

Host: The Pace Peace Center, Pace University School of Law

List of Participants

1) From the Pace Peace Center:

Benjamin B.Ferencz, Executive Director, Graduate of Harvard Law School. Adjunct Professor of International Law, former Nuremberg war crimes Prosecutor, author of many books and articles dealing with the law of peace.

Gertrude Ferencz, Special Assistant to the Executive Director.

Prof. Nicholas Robinson, Peace Center Supervisory Committee, Professor of Environmental Law. Authority on legal problems of the environment.

Paul Szasz, Peace Center U.N. Liaison, Adjunct Professor, former Director UN Office of Legal Counsel. Author of many books and articles on international law.

Sandra Bendfeldt, Program Director; graduate of Pace Law School.

Dr. Rose Cooper, Video Project Director.

Richard Duffee, Bibliography Project Director, candidate for Certificate in International Law, Pace Law School.

2) From the Institute of State and Law, Moscow:

Dr. Galina Shinkaretskaya, Specialist on International Courts.

Prof. Rais A. Touzmohammad, Leading Research Fellow, Member of Presidium, Soviet Lawyers Association.

3) From the Institute of State and Law, Ukranian Academy of Sciences, Kiev.

Prof. Yuri S. Shemshouchenko, Director of the Institute. Author of almost 200 scientific publications including ten books dealing with the problems of the environment.

Dr. Vladimir V. Furkalo, Deputy Chief, Department of Foreign Relations, Academy of Science of the Ukrainian SSR. Author of several books and authority on arms control and the law of armed conflict.

Dr. Vladimir I. Evintov, Senior Research Fellow in International Law. Author of several books including ***International Community and Legal Order*** (Kiev, 1990).

4) From the United Nations and Non-Governmental Organizations.

Robert Muller, Chancellor of the University for Peace, Former Asst. Secretary-General of the UN, Winner of UNESCO Peace Prize, noted peace lecturer and author.

Jack Yost, UN Representative, World Association of World Federation.

Richard Hudson, Executive Director, Center for War/Peace Studies.

Lucy Webster, UN Department of Disarmament Affairs.

5) Guests who did not participate in the discussion:

W.H. Ferry, Peace Activist, Board of directors of the Exploratory Project on the Conditions for Peace (EXPRO).

Gerald Mische, Founder and co-President of Global Education Associates.

Britt Kjolstad, United Nations Law Librarian.

B.G. Ramcharan, UN Office of Research and Information.

Sergei Tarassenko, United Nations Office of Legal Affairs.

Introductory Dialogue: International Law and Order

Participants:

Prof. Benjamin B. Ferencz
Executive Director, Pace University School of Law Peace Center; Former Prosecutor, Nuremberg War Crimes Trials; Professor of Law, Pace University School of Law

Prof. Rais A. Touzmohammad
Leading Research Fellow, Member of Presidium, Soviet Lawyer's Association

---

Prof. Benjamin B. Ferencz

Our preliminary agenda called for all of the conference participants to begin consideration of a new legal framework for a more rational global society where the force of law would replace the law of force. I suggested that we focus on three areas:

LAWS to set forth minimum standards of international conduct;

COURTS to determine if the minimum standards of international conduct have been violated and to serve as a forum for judicial settlement of disputes; and

EFFECTIVE INTERNATIONAL LAW ENFORCEMENT. May I ask you whether this agenda and broad framework seems a suitable basis for discussion?

Prof. Rais A. Touzmohammad: Yes, from a jurisprudential point of view it seems very good indeed, but nevertheless, I have certain doubts. If we look at history we can ask whether international law really reflects the rules of behavior followed by those who deal with international affairs. Can you really equate international law with domestic national law? I doubt it. There *should* be laws and courts and a mechanism for enforcement internationally but as long as we are operating under a system of state sovereignty the approach you suggest is very problematical on all three points. Perhaps we can talk about implementation rather than enforcement if we are to look to our respective governments for acceptance of our ideas. For the time being you are ahead of the public view of the situation.

Prof. Benjamin B. Ferencz: I quite agree that what I have outlined is far ahead of its time. You are quite right in your implied criticism when you suggest that under today's conditions one cannot equate international law with national law. The existence of the sovereign state is the main barrier to that. Even those relatively few norms of international behavior which are accepted are too vague. We also agree that the prevailing international courts do not resemble local national courts and that the peaceful settlement of disputes internationally remains not the work of lawyers but largely the work of diplomats concerned with mediation and negotiation. Nor do we have, under the present system, the legal ability to enforce laws in a world society composed of states which declare themselves to be the ultimate sovereign authority regarding their own decisions or actions. You may be correct in suggesting that we talk about implementation rather than enforcement. What I am suggesting however is that we consider methods of changing the contemporary, and in my view, unsatisfactory and dangerous situation.

Let us assume for purposes of our discussion that the problem of sovereignty will be overcome and that states will recognize in the face of a nuclear threat that in the year 1990 and thereafter it is necessary to adjust and change the system. They must yield some of their sovereignty in order to protect themselves. They must voluntarily adjust the structure to meet the needs of the hi-tech and nuclear world and that it is for their own interest and protection. I don't think that the doubts which you correctly expressed should stop us.

The work that we do here may serve as a foundation stone so that those who may deal with these problems in years to come will not have to start from scratch. Let us begin to think about these problems now and exchange views in the hope that those who control the world will benefit from it when they are ready to deal with it. Let us try to overcome the obstacles which you have described.

Prof. Rais A. Touzmohammad: I fully agree with the general approach but let's not assume that the terms you used actually reflect the existing reality. We need more than norms; we need laws which are enforceable - which is not the case now. For example, the Soviet Union invaded Afghanistan and the United States invaded Grenada and there were no laws to stop them.

Prof. Benjamin B. Ferencz: True, those actions would normally be considered aggression and under the principles of the Nuremberg Charter and Tribunal aggression was the most serious crime. At that time, both the Soviet Union and the United States felt that it was a legal and human obligation to make future aggression impossible. When the United Nations reached a consensus definition of aggression in 1974, after many years of effort, making the prohibition really effective was blocked by the problem you mention. States were unwilling to surrender their sovereignty or the right to decide for themselves when they might attack their neighbor. Thus, they reserved to themselves the right of "self defense" and that meant that all future wars of aggression would be fought only in "self defense." The legal definition which was supposed to codify the international norm that attacking your neighbor was impermissible didn't really stop anyone. Many nations have committed aggression since then.

It seems to me that the first thing that lawyers can do is to say to the heads of state: "You are not serious in your professed declaration that states should be prohibited from committing aggression. If you are not ready to outlaw acts of aggression you will pay the price and it will be an increasingly higher price. The next time it may cost the life of every living thing on this planet. You must therefore recognize that it is in your own interest to prevent that from happening. You must therefore really accept certain minimum norms as binding law." Such action is now necessary to preserve the nation state itself as well as life on this planet.

3

We should therefore try now to take a legal step forward. For example, leaving aside for the moment the question of self defense, the definition of aggression and other conventions purporting to curb the use of force, (such as the convention against terrorism), reaffirm the principle that "nothing in this convention shall prevent attempts to obtain self determination or freedom from colonial oppression or alien domination" or words to that effect. These are goals which the international community has correctly declared to be worthwhile and lawful. But as long as you have written such exceptions into the codification of law, the attempts to restrain the use of force will be meaningless. One principle contradicts the other and there is no clarification. Looking at such an instrument as a lawyer, I say that a document with such a large loophole is worthless as a restraint. Do you agree?

Prof. Rais A. Touzmohammad: I think that is relevant but I would like to add that lawyers have a professional goal to work out laws that bind the subjects but international law has certain special peculiarities. Let us start our agenda with discussing the principles or norms of international law. The precepts of human values that are recognized as *jus cogens* are somewhat abstract from real life. They must be related to the precepts that really concern human beings and perhaps we can formulate new principles along such lines. We could close loopholes and reach principles of greater interest to humanity. Although there is a tremendous growth of the system of international law, we are also witnessing new forms of behavior by superpowers which still rely on the use of force.

I agree that it's time to make clearer definitions but what are the guarantees that those who are supposed to be bound will actually give up the use of force? There may be disarmament but new forms of force may appear such as economic force and technological force and these must also be brought under international control. We should insert that in our considerations.

That is a reality which has to be taken into account. The future which you write about in your books, and particular in your book *Planethood*, does not see the role of peoples organized as national ethnic groups or non-governmental groups as a rising influence. Can they become a real subject of international law? Can they help in working out the principles of international law and in enforcing it by influencing the governments involved? Their role in the future international law is rising and cannot be ignored as it has in the past. That is a reality regardless of the form of government since governments are their own bureaucratic and political systems and don't consider the interests of the people as an independent group with a voice of its own Peoples as subjects of international law.

Prof. Benjamin B. Ferencz: You have covered the entire panorama of our agenda and I welcome that expansion of our frame of reference. You have noted that certain widely accepted norms of behavior are graced by a Latin phrase *jus cogens* to give them an aura of validity, but even these norms are vague and there are no guarantees of enforcement. Surely economic power, as you note, can constitute a form of aggression and there must be some broadening of the concept of aggression itself. You raise the fundamental question of the relationship of individuals and governments and that affects implementation. Individuals deserve the sanctification in international law which enables them to prevail against their governments if their interests are ignored. To synthesize what you have said we must recall that everything is interrelated and interconnected and must move forward as a system to become acceptable.

The emergence of new norms is a slow process, e.g. the inclusion of international economic rights and obligations is not in the definition of aggression or the current draft of Crimes against the Peace and Security of Mankind. Yet, at the United Nations, states have started to talk about a New Economic Order, which raises the question whether all human beings are entitled to certain minimum standards such as the right to life, food, water and shelter which are economic norms which have not yet been accepted by the international community but are being discussed because there is realization of the accuracy of what you are saying about the need to clarify and grant such entitlement to all.

We must think about the terms of expanding the role of the individual. We are already seeing the protection of such rights e.g. the Court of Human Rights of the European Community allows the individual to take his own government to an international court for violating his rights under the European Convention on Human Rights. In each case the government must answer in a court of law for violating a right granted by law to individuals. International enforcement is still lacking in the sense I suggested, yet decisions are accepted because the governments recognize the need to abide by rules they themselves have laid down in their common interest. We see the individual coming into his own rights. It is reflective of a growing trend among enlightened and democratic societies. Individuals are rebelling and insisting upon their common rights.

But we must recall that there are certain dangers. [United States Supreme Court Justice] Holmes noted that freedom is not unlimited: "My right to swing my arms ends where your nose begins." Freedom must also respect the rights of others. We must use the domestic society as a model for the international model. The United States formed a union of states, as did the Soviet Union and others, where rights were granted to a central body to the extent necessary to make the society function yet other rights were retained by the component parts. The form of government must be made tolerable yet adequate to meet specific needs. You are right to say that the role of the people is rising. Our function as lawyers is to encourage the people in their striving and to give them guidance.

You have said privately: "We are building the banks of a river through which new waters must flow." We are building the banks of that river by human beings everywhere asserting his or her fundamental rights for food, shelter, family, recreation etc. Today, some have more advantages than they can use. There is no reason why others should have so little. Let us as lawyers lay out the plan for the banks through which new waters may flow so that a more just society can be created in a peaceful way. Without law there will be chaos and with chaos you will have bloodshed on a scale never before seen. That is the challenge which we face together.

In our approach we must begin with step one and do the best we can and then move on to each additional step, knowing that they are all connected and that no one step by itself will produce our desired goal. If we do that, I think we can convince the leaders and the people that it is in everybody's interest and we can make a constructive contribution.

Prof. Rais A. Touzmohammad: When I speak of peoples I mean the sum of individuals. They are entitled to be subjects of international law. That also includes minorities. We are trying to organize a conference of minorities in Europe to deal with their special problems. In many countries international lawyers have forgotten that state sovereignty is derived from the sovereignty of peoples as such. The peoples must be regarded as substantial subjects of law.

Prof. Benjamin B. Ferencz: I agree that the sovereignty of the King derives from the people. He is there to serve the people as the ultimate beneficiary of society; they are the substance of what we are dealing with.

Let us move on and consider the United Nations Charter which spoke in the name of "We the Peoples" and let us see where it has worked well and where it hasn't and what we can do as lawyers to try to improve it to meet the needs of the 21st century.

Reevaluating Existing Legal Mechanisms

Prof. Benjamin B. Ferencz: If we make the assumption that governments have asked for our help in building structures for peace and are now wiling to make the changes necessary for a peaceful world, where would you begin?

Prof. Rais A. Touzmohammad: I would begin with what we have already achieved. We may be proud as international lawyers that governments particularly after World War II managed to reach agreements on certain norms which had been evolving throughout history but which have now reached the status of imperative norms which cannot be changed without agreement of all of the subjects of international relations and which bind all of them. They have been accepted by consensus; such as in the Declaration of Principles of International Law Governing Friendly Relations Among States accepted by the General Assembly in 1970. A United Nations Special Committee worked for more than 6 years to achieve that. It represents a platform from which to move into the 21st century.

Principles which were fixed in the Charter are being elaborated. We thus have both a moral and legal basis as a starting point. We may add additional principles formulated in the Final Helsinki Act of 1975 which was ratified by 35 nations. These are basic. Naturally the situation has changed somewhat in the last 25 years and there may be some modification needed to meet contemporary needs.

Prof. Benjamin B. Ferencz: You are right in pointing out that the international community has already come quite a long way toward establishing a legal foundation for friendly relations among nations and it is not necessary now to start from scratch. The declarations to which you refer can be supplemented by the Manila Declaration and a host of conventions defining human rights and permissible and impermissible acts. We can take them as our starting points but there are difficulties with those instruments which should be addressed.

Two fundamental difficulties are that such instruments are ambiguous; the terminology used in order to reach consensus was often deliberately vague so that each party could interpret it for its own interests and secondly they did not set up a mechanism or agency to resolve differences in interpretation of these vague instruments. Often the principles stated are contradictory. For example: aggression is prohibited but self defense is allowable. The use of force is not allowed but humanitarian intervention may be permissible. If you put some of these principles next to other inconsistent principles of equal validity then you recognize a shortcoming in our legal system which needs correction if we are to be more effective. What do you think about that?

Prof. Rais A. Touzmohammad: Let me first address your question about who may be the judge in case the basic principles conflict and clash with each other. I think there should be certain mechanisms which now do not exist internationally and we may have to look to domestic models. For example, in the United States you have a Supreme Court to decide whether laws conflict with the constitution. In Europe, you have the Constitutional Court of the Federal Republic of Germany. A similar body exists in France and in the Soviet Union. In the course of our reforms to create a more democratic system we created a Committee for Constitutional Supervision. We may look to these as samples or we may look toward the United Nations which has its ultimate legal organ in the International Court of Justice. Its Statute would, of course, require certain modifications.

The International Court of Justice only deals with legal disputes brought before the court but only States can bring such disputes. The Courts of Human Rights may be more relevant since they deal with conflicts between individuals and governments or between the citizen and the state. If peoples and minorities are to play an increasing part in international relations, the idea of an international court must be expanded to give them jurisdiction to deal with clashes of principles which may affect their rights. The Court should be composed of authoritative personalities well known in the international community so that they enjoy the respect of the peoples.

Prof. Benjamin B. Ferencz: You are suggesting that rather than trying to improve and clarify the existing laws that we accept them as they are and turn to an independent third body for the purpose of interpreting the clauses which appear to be in conflict. Your reference to the possibility of using the International Court of Justice or the existing courts of human rights in Strasbourg and Costa Rica are very useful suggestions for moving forward quickly.

We would still have to wait for States to take the initiative and this may be a serious obstacle. Do you think it would accelerate progress even more if the Secretary General of the United Nations were to be authorized to request Advisory Opinions of the Court as he can do now under the Charter but address his requests to these ambiguities and request interpretations as it applies to a particular situation. The Secretary General does not have to wait for states to request such action or get involved in disputes about whether the Court has jurisdiction or not. The Secretary General can turn to the Court and say: State A has invaded State B. B says its aggression, A says it's self defense. Here are the facts as we have been able to ascertain them; what is your opinion? The same could apply to other ambiguities such as whether its impermissible intervention or allowable humanitarian intervention or whether its self determination or rebellion or secession. Do you think such an innovation would make matters easier and be useful?

Prof. Rais A. Touzmohammad: Let me first make an observation. I must agree that some of the declarations I mentioned, in order to reach consensus, had certain compromises and loopholes. Even if the wordings were perfect, the changes in the world since then would require modifications to be responsive to the new challenges.

Prof. Benjamin B. Ferencz: That is a very useful suggestion. Of course the law is not static. It must keep changing to meet the needs of changing times. Principles declared 200 years ago, as in the United States Constitution and various human rights declarations, today are interpreted by the prevailing courts in ways which the framers never anticipated at the time. The law, like every living thing, changes all the time. You are right that codifications of law are not set in concrete for all time. Let's accept that as being beyond dispute.

Prof. Rais A. Touzmohammad: May I also express my opinion on your main question about the Secretary General. I think it's a very good suggestion, but experience in domestic and international life has demonstrated that vesting executive power in one hand generates a momentum and motive for it to become overwhelming. The post of the Secretary General may itself become a decision maker above the power of State members and may generate new difficulties. The General Assembly should also be authorized to seek advisory opinions from the International Court of Justice to reduce that threat. I would also give more rights to the Security Council.

Prof. Benjamin B. Ferencz: I accept your point. I did not mean that to be an exclusive right of the Secretary General. I share your concern about putting too much power in one hand. We must have a system of checks and balances. Enforcement would still rest with the Security Council so there is some check on both the Secretary General and the International Court of Justice. Incidentally, Prof. Louis Sohn of Harvard, now of Georgia, has made such a suggestion for expanded use of advisory opinions. I have not had a chance yet to discuss it with him in detail but my feeling is also that the authority to request opinions should be as broad as possible.

Let us put aside for the moment the problem of making the General Assembly, the Security Council or the International Court of Justice more effective and focus on law itself as the first leg of a three legged stool (law, courts and enforcement) on which international society must sit. I think we have agreed that we should take as our beginning the existing and established norms the *jus cogens* and treat it as though it were binding law even though these norms may not have been codified. Codification might make it simpler and easier for people to understand.

Let us include in our scan all of the existing instruments, whether they be declarations or consensus resolutions or treaties or whatever, which define the fundamental human rights such as those to which you have referred: The Friendly Relations Declaration, the Helsinki Accords, the Manila Declaration and the new ones which will come in the future ; the rights of secession for example or the right to breathe fresh air or have fresh drinking water etc. Law is there to protect the human rights of people everywhere. The great American Declaration of Independence proclaimed that all humans (I won't repeat all *men* since women also have the same rights) are created equal and are endowed with certain unalienable rights. By the way, the United States Constitution did not recognize rights of women or of slaves. But let us assume now that *all* humans have certain fundamental rights. If you had to begin today, which rights would you list as being fundamental?

Prof. Rais A. Touzmohammad: Rights have changed since the American and French revolutions. Nowadays, as you have correctly noted in many of your publications, humanity is becoming united because of objective reasons. The first right is the right to life; the right to live. This is the most substantial right. There is a new right recognized by the United Nations in 1986, the right to development. It is very comprehensive since it covers individuals, peoples and states and all fields. There must be a good environment, and there must be the possibility for the individual to develop his capacity as a specimen biologically, intellectually, God knows what. There is also the important right of any person to be defended by courts and other institutions; to be defended by fair trial and by law. This right does not exist in many countries.

In the Soviet Union, for example, even now individuals are not accustomed to seeking such rights in either criminal or civil procedures. The same is true in other countries. In contrast, when a person is assaulted in the United States, it is customary and natural for him to turn to the courts for help. These rights are essential for a progressive future in which the people can live safely. Another right which has already been mentioned by you and many bodies, is freedom from hunger.

Prof. Benjamin B. Ferencz: It was President Roosevelt who spoke of four freedoms; freedom from want, fear, freedom of speech and religion. These were fundamental.

Prof. Rais A. Touzmohammad: There are others, naturally. Freedom from fear may be more important today even than it was in Roosevelt's time.

Prof. Benjamin B. Ferencz: I think, without taking the time now to list them all, that we can agree that there are certain fundamental entitlements that all should share. You have mentioned some of them, basic human rights to life, peace, development of the human being to his maximum potential, the right to be defended if he is accused, fair trial.

Many human rights instruments spell out many of those rights. The important thing for us as lawyers is to begin to put them all together in one shape or another and declare that these are rights which the international community has already affirmed in one way or another and the time has come now for serious lawyers from different cultures and different parts of the world to agree upon at least these minimum rights. They can be expanded later to include other rights as the international community gets ready to accept them.

I would certainly accept as a starting point the right to life, the right to food, to clean air, to water, to minimum medical services, the right to some literacy, some basic education as part of what you referred to as development. These are surely fundamental things and if lawyers cannot define these we are not doing our job. The function of law is to define for the community what their obligations and rights are. I think we can do that.

Let us now shift our focus away from these basic individual human rights which are fundamental since we should be protecting the individual above all. Let us deal with the rights and obligations of states and let us consider the tension between the notions of aggression and self defense.

At Nuremberg we thought we were taking a great step forward when we declared that the crime of aggressive war was a punishable international crime because it encompassed all other crimes; robbery, rape, pillage, murder etc... all committed on an enormous scale. It was Justice Jackson, the American Chief Prosecutor, who said that it would be absurd to punish only the petty crimes of little people and the big crimes of big people are ignored. He said: "The time has come for the law to take a step forward."

Aggressive war was declared to be a Crime against Peace. This was accepted by the General Assembly of the United Nations unanimously and we hoped that it would become part of law. But it didn't work out that way. It was accepted by the British, the Soviet Union, the French and generally accepted as *desirable* and something we had to have. But the United Nations Charter in Article 51 said that self defense was permissible. That was a principle that went back to ancient days.

14

Now in the nuclear age perhaps we ought to change that. As lawyers, perhaps we should say that self defense is NOT permissible - a very radical thought. I take the point from General Douglas MacArthur who told the defeated Japanese after the war that they would never be allowed to defend themselves again; they would be permanently disarmed. He wrote their constitution which in effect said they would not be allowed to spend money for armaments. Japan would have to depend upon the international community to defend it in case of unjustified attack. Because Japanese aggression was considered so terrible, the international community would never again be subjected to such a risk.

The result of that was that the Japanese spent their money on building new machines and got very wealthy and prosperous and were not endangered by the rest of the community. They lived happily and prosperously ever after. It was a wonderful thing. I am raising the question of whether this hallowed notion of self defense should remain. Perhaps we should rely on another agency for the defense of the law. If a thief enters your house you may defend yourself under certain circumstances but you cannot run after him and kill him. You must call the police and bring him to court. Maybe the time has come to change things internationally.

The United Nations Charter said a nation could only defend itself under restricted conditions. It could only do so temporarily until the Security Council could intervene. Today the Council can intervene within two minutes. There is immediate communication so we don't need the old system. Maybe the time has come to eliminate the right of self defense. Is that too radical an idea for a radical from the Soviet Union?

Prof. Rais A. Touzmohammad: It's an interesting question. Art. 51 of the United Nations Charter expressly stipulates that in case of aggression nations have the right of self defense. At the same time there is an obligation to inform the Security Council which must intervene. When the United States at Dumbarton Oaks and at San Francisco proposed the self defense article for the Charter, the Soviet Union came forward with the restriction. The case you gave from domestic criminal law of defense against a thief only until the police arrives solved that problem domestically.

But if you are talking about international law for the 21st century which we are considering, naturally, if certain other circumstances prevail, the right of self defense will be irrelevant. But what is required first is full disarmament, and the ideas of *Planethood* about which you wrote must prevail where all the people in all countries are not only politically but also legally educated and have moral standards high enough not to let their governments violate this new peaceful law which mandates the non use of force even in self defense.

Prof. Benjamin B. Ferencz: You are right. But Article 51 of the Charter allows individual or collective self defense only if an *armed attack* occurs and is further limited by time only until the Security Council can act and it must immediately be reported to the Security Council. Yet we know from experience that it didn't work. If an American soldier is stopped at a check point and is shot because he runs through the check point, that is seen as an armed attack against the United States and justifies not only our invasion of the offending country (Panama) but calling all of our allies to join us as well. I don't think that leads to a very peaceful world.

I don't think that was in the minds of the Charter framers. If we as lawyers know that it hasn't worked then we must try to change the instrument somehow to make it work. I think we both seem to be agreed that in the future we must look for some more effective legal means of preventing the possibility of any state deciding for itself when it may use force under the pretext of self defense or vital interests or whatever it may be.

Prof. Rais A. Touzmohammad: As we did in Afghanistan.

Prof. Benjamin B. Ferencz: We all do it and have been doing it but it's much too dangerous to continue doing it in the 21st century. Let us in our future discussion see what we can do about it and have the optimistic hope that we can come up with something more effective than what was done 40 or more years ago.

Conference joined by:

Dr. Galina Shinkaretskaya.
Senior Researcher, Institute of State and Law, Moscow

Prof. Paul Szasz.
former Director of the United Nations Office of the Legal Counsel; Adjunct Professor of International Law, Pace University School of Law

Sandra Bendfeldt.
Attorney; Program Director, Pace Peace Center

Richard Duffee.
Assistant, Pace Peace Center; Candidate for Certificate in International Law, Pace University School of Law.

Gertrude Ferencz:
Assistant to the Executive Director, Pace Peace Center.

Problems Posed by State Sovereignty

Prof. Benjamin B. Ferencz: Let us continue our basic discussion of some of the objectives of the conference and some of the fundamental problems we face in trying to restructure international society along legal and rational lines. We have already informally reviewed the dialogue which I had with Prof. Touzmohammad and I would now like to ask Galina: How do we overcome the problems of state sovereignty, how do we begin and where do we go?

Dr. Galina Shinkaretskaya: I think this is the most up-to-date topic which faces our world now. To have a legal order in the world and to have sound and proper conditions for people, we must organize three elements. The first is the need for all people to understand the dangers facing the world and the ways they must behave in order to eliminate those dangers. There is need for a spirit of collaboration among all of the units which exist in the world. This covers not merely states but all sorts of societies, associations and individuals. Individuals are, after all, the main goal of all the social sciences and the efforts made by states and statesmen.

The second element is the situation inside the countries. When we consider how decisions are made by statesmen we can see that what happens within the country itself is decisive. The main thing is to promote the rule-of-law. As I can judge from the experience in my own country, statesmen are unable to take proper external foreign policy decisions until statesmen are rule-of-law minded. Without that basis they cannot decide in ways which are good for other people or even people within their own country. Enhancing legal education is one of the main functions of international scholars and lawyers.

The third element is the legal mechanisms. This is perhaps the easiest to define. It is here that we international lawyers can do something. We can propagate the idea of introducing new legal mechanisms into international life and then we can press our own statesmen and decisionmakers to act in the direction of promoting these new legal mechanisms. I am convinced that we international lawyers must work on all three elements. What we need is a good network. If we have a good network of people who share our ideas, and there are plenty throughout the world, if we can find and make contact with them we can all work together and discuss our ideas and promote them so that they can become a reality.

Prof. Benjamin B. Ferencz: Let me just ask for clarification on a point. You have stressed the requirement that there be an awareness of what the problems in the world are, and also that we have to understand the conditions as they exist in each state; some may be more amenable to the rule of law than others. In addition to education of the public and setting up a network of persons who are prepared to follow this rule of law, you have stressed the need for what you call new "legal mechanisms." Do you have in mind new institutions, improved institutions or do you also have in mind the clarification of existing norms through a process of codification or treaties or some other legal *paper* mechanisms to achieve these goals?

Dr. Galina Shinkaretskaya: What I mean is all sorts of mechanisms which exist now and which can be created. There are, for example, permanent mechanisms like the United Nations, or associations. There are also committees which deal with specific topics and when the item is completed the conference dies. There may be informal actions, like people from different countries joining together for a march or public demonstration for peace. This is part of what we call people's diplomacy. I consider these also a peacemaking mechanism.

Prof. Benjamin B. Ferencz: You are saying that we must really be flexible in the various types of mechanisms we use.

Dr. Galina Shinkaretskaya: That's right.

Prof. Benjamin B. Ferencz: Paul Szasz, you have had vast experience at the United Nations, how do you think we can approach these problems in a constructive way?

Paul Szasz: The original question was how we can organize peace rationally in a world of sovereign states. The answer is: "You can't." As long as states remain sovereign, you cannot have a rational system that leads to peace. By sovereign I mean that in effect a state can do what it wants.

The only possibility is to erode that sovereignty until it becomes less and less and finally, in effect, disappears in the same way as the states in the United States still call themselves sovereign but, of course, they are not sovereign in any real sense of the word. That erosion of national sovereignty has already started. It will still take some time and we don't know how long it will take. The longer it takes the longer we will be exposed to the dangers of war.

What sort of erosion can take place? One is that states more and more have to be controlled by international law. There has to be more international law in more areas. The mechanisms for creating that international law through multilateral treaties, and acceleration of the process of formulating international customary law is already in place. It just has to be exercised. Similarly, states have to have their sovereignty eroded by agreeing more and more to execution of international agreements and the supervision of international obligations. Thirdly states have to agree more and more to settle their disputes through international courts. To the extent that they do that with fewer and fewer reservations, that too will erode their sovereignty and increase the chances for a rational world peace.

Institutions to cause these changes are largely already in existence. You have the United Nations and the United Nations system and, to some extent, regional organizations and systems. They are by no means perfect and we can discuss their imperfections later. Basically the systems are in place although some important changes might improve their functioning.

Prof. Benjamin B. Ferencz: That's very helpful, Paul. I hope that we can discuss techniques for accelerating the erosion of sovereign power that interferes with peace and improving the various institutions which we have. Why don't we begin by considering the United Nations itself, which I think represents the furthest point reached by humankind in erecting an institution for peace.

Improving the United Nations Charter

Professor Benjamin B. Ferencz: The Charter grew out of the necessities generated by the inability of the Covenant of the League of Nations to prevent World War II. The shock and tragedy of that war increased the determination of states to try to prevent war from recurring. Nevertheless, looking back at it more than 40 years later, we find that it hasn't worked; at least not in the area of international security. Wars have continued. How do you make the Charter binding law and how do you make the institution of the United Nations stronger and more useful in eroding state sovereignty and in becoming generally accepted?

Paul Szasz: I don't see how you can make the Charter much stronger. It's as strong as it has to be. The instrument for security, the Security Council, has all of the powers that could possibly be needed to fulfill its purposes. The difficulty, of course, is that states are still much too sovereign to yield to international law and international organizations in those cases that they consider important for their own preservation. There are, unfortunately, far too many instances in which states consider a matter important enough to supersede international law.

The only reason the relevant provisions of the Charter have not operated well in the postwar period was, in effect, the cold war. The Security Council was paralyzed by vetoes from one side or another during the East-West confrontation. One could discuss doing away with the veto, but that's somewhat like doing away with the brake in a car. It isn't going to function. The world is not ready for a veto-less Council or to accept a majority, or even a qualified majority, on decisions or questions of life and death for nations.

The way the Security Council really works requires that a great deal of negotiation take place for a consensus to be reached as to how a particular problem can be solved. That process may take years or decades, but unless such a resolution is reached in the Security Council, the problem cannot be resolved peacefully. That need not be a perpetual state of affairs. Once sovereignty has eroded in a sufficient number of states, the Council can be strengthened.

The only changes that I think could be considered at this point would be minor changes in the composition of the Council and the states to which vetoes should be attributed. But the main characteristics: that the most powerful states should represent the Security Council, that at least some of them should have a veto, (possibly even some regions should have vetoes) and that there be a reasonable high majority for taking decisions, should not be changed.

Prof. Benjamin B. Ferencz: You have described a very realistic picture of the situation as it exists today and pointed to a possible future direction. Can we as international lawyers recommend improvements which we think are rational even though we know that they may not be acceptable to states today?

Even if you extend the veto power to other states because the power structures have changed since 1945 aren't you still supporting a mechanism whereby one state can block any progress in the security field? Would that be a rational system? If you are looking for a consensus among 160 nations, or even a more limited bloc, you are allowing one nation to prevent any progress until consensus may be reached possibly decades later, as you say. Can the world simply wait? Are we as lawyers going to recommend that we continue that system even though we recognize it to be deficient?

Paul Szasz: There are some improvements one could recommend. I think the veto has to be kept for those decisions of the Council that in effect activate the collective power of the world community; particularly those set forth in Articles 41 and 42 (enforcement sanctions) of the Charter. Certainly the use of collective military force cannot be mobilized against the wish of those states or groups that should be able to use the veto. On the other hand, one might be able to change the San Francisco formula as to what is "veto-able," to reduce that area considerably. For example, condemnations of the Council that some state is wrong in having started a military action might not necessarily be subject to a veto. Thus, determinations under Art. 39 of Chap. VII (determination of threats to the peace or aggression) could be exempted from veto.

Another area that might be exempted from veto or might be obtainable by a slight amendment to the Charter would be to require states to submit disputes to peaceful settlement under Art.33 and perhaps even require a submission to judicial settlement by the International Court of Justice. These would lead to legal or arbitral determinations to supplement the political determinations under my previous suggestion as to the rights and wrongs of certain countries in particular conflicts. That would not necessarily eliminate those conflicts, nevertheless states are very sensitive to being publicly and collectively said to be in the wrong. That is, for example, the reason why the United States has vetoed the resolutions regarding its actions in Panama and Grenada and the Soviet Union vetoed the resolutions concerning the Soviet invasion of Afghanistan. States don't like to be condemned by international organizations and if they can prevent it they will. If they can't prevent it, one might hope that in certain instances they would conform. Lawyers could recommend such changes in the Charter provisions.

Prof. Benjamin B. Ferencz: The veto power was first put in because nations were not prepared to accept any outside decision regarding the use of its own military forces. The Chinese representative, Wellington Koo, noted at that time that it was not a rational system but neither the Russians nor the Americans were prepared to allow their boys to be sent back to war on the decision of someone else. But you have suggested that certain progress may still be possible. If peaceful settlement could be made mandatory, and if we could place armaments under international control, would that be a direction in which we could move toward a more peaceful legal structure?

Prof. Rais A. Touzmohammad: Unfortunately, we are living in a world which we hope is just beginning to pass from the today's realistic principle of balance of power to a balance of interests. This is just being proclaimed by scholars and peoples, particularly in recognition of the new dangers to humanity as a whole. We are just at the start and therefore the foreseeable future for this century will still be based on military or other balance of power principles.

If we look at the history of attempts to revise the United Nations Charter, a Perestroika of the Charter, we see that the balance of power is still there. The majority of United Nations members are against the veto. The whole nonaligned movement is strictly against it. They have formal objections against parts which they say have nothing to do with democracy, such as the provisions that five powers (the Permanent Members) may decide against them. The problem is there even though those countries may, for the time being, be silenced by the diplomatic efforts of the big powers. They have to be taken into consideration. To convert the Charter into a code of principles or of law would require a change that recognizes the balance of interests of all participating countries.

If we are to make the United Nations Charter into a code of norms that have the effect of law similar to domestic law, it must include those codification of principles which have already been reached at the United Nations. We have at least 40 such treaties, conventions etc. which codify certain principle laid down by the United Nations since 1945.

As for the Security Council, I fully agree with Paul that this is not the time for drastic changes. The nonaligned nations are insisting that the membership of the Security Council must be enlarged. They figured out that if the Council could be enlarged to include 90 members then in effect the veto power would pass to the nonaligned. To get rid of the veto power and have decisions reached by majority vote would be a democratic principle. To bring the Council up to date, one would have to take into account the role of peoples as such. These are not represented in the Council at all, neither by states nor as members despite the fact that the United Nations Charter was accepted in the name of "The Peoples."

We should recall from history, e.g.the American revolution, that state sovereignty is a secondary one - it is derived from the sovereignty of the people. But in practice, in many non-democratic societies, the bureaucracy has the upper hand. The people are subordinated. The interests of the people must be reflected directly in the international system.

States understand this situation. For example, about 2 years ago the Soviet Union proposed that the nonaligned movement as such had to be represented in the Security Council. This reflects the awareness of the changing situation in the world, at least by one of the superpowers. But they have not yet gone as far as to support the idea that the *peoples* should be directly represented in the Council.

Prof. Benjamin B. Ferencz: This is a pretty sharp criticism of the present system. It has been pointed out that it's a system based upon power rather than concern for common interests and it's undemocratic because only five powers have usurped for themselves more rights than anybody else. The nonaligned nations object to it; in fact probably everybody who doesn't have a veto power objects to it. Rais says this is not representative of the people but only of states and governments whose interests are not always the same as the interests of the peoples. Even non-governmental organizations have no special role in this structure. Galina, what do you think of that?

Dr. Galina Shinkaretskaya: Whatever we may say, every person is the product of his own society, and I speak as a representative of Soviet society. The main contradiction in the world as we can see from inside the Soviet Union is the need for democratization which will allow individuals to express and to be themselves.

In my country today we can see two contradictory things: first the state is a bureaucratic organization which hampers the normal living of the human being. At the same time, the state as a bureaucratic organization becomes the forum for expression of the will of the people. For example, if we take the recent decision of the Supreme Soviets of Russia or Moldavia - the national declarations of independence from the Soviet Union - these express the genuine will of their nations and of their people. Sometimes the state may be bureaucratic but sometimes that bureaucracy becomes the best vehicle for expressing what the people really want. The same is true of the United Nations.

When the United Nations was created, it expressed the genuine will of the nations fighting Fascism. The lofty ideas and slogans written into the Charter expressed the will of the nations. But when the states began to implement them into legal norms, they sought to insert their own interests into the Charter and that may be why the Charter reflects so much of the bureaucratic ideas of the state. As a Soviet, I can see that contradiction as one of the main problems in the international field but I don't see how we can solve it.

Prof. Benjamin B. Ferencz: You are apparently agreeing with Rais that the present United Nations structure is undemocratic in that it has unfair representation and that it's unfair to the people, who resent the states speaking for them without giving them a chance to speak for themselves. In states where the people have been treated as wards of the state they now seek a freedom to express their own opinion. There are some suggestions that there should be a Second Assembly of the Non-governmental Organizations representing the people more directly.

Prof. Rais A. Touzmohammad: The people still have great hope in the United Nations.

Prof. Benjamin B. Ferencz: Isn't it time after almost 50 years of this prototype to reexamine it and convene another Dumbarton Oaks conference where the people will be represented, where the Non-governmental Organizations will be represented, the nonaligned will be represented, to see if we can reach agreement on a more democratic instrument more reflective of the needs of the 21st century?

Richard Duffee: I agree completely. I have always been a fan of Gary Davis, who had a good idea in 1948 of trying to become a World Citizen and applying for admission himself in the United Nations. The United Nations should have some means for representing individuals. We could have another Dumbarton Oaks conference but the crucial decision would be how to determine who would be invited. Whoever determines that is in control of the conference. The ground rules would have to be considered over a long period of time.

Prof. Benjamin B. Ferencz: Rais, wouldn't it be a good thing for the nonaligned movement with which you are closely associated and where you are now trying to organize the Non-governmental Organizations in a more effective way to take the initiative and call for a new Dumbarton Oaks, not in Washington DC but in more neutral territory, to reexamine this instrument which will be 50 years old soon to see if it meets the new needs of the times? Perhaps they could make their own proposals about how it needs to be changed in order to be reflective of their interests, rather than just power and the needs which we have for a peaceful international society.

Prof. Rais A. Touzmohammad: I fully support your idea, but there are difficulties. The Non-governmental Organizations in the nonaligned countries are not yet adequately organized. They can support the idea once they have become more effective which I hope will be the case. But the nonaligned states themselves are not likely to be helpful. Within the United Nations, they have participated in the Special Committee on the Charter. Under pressure from the major powers they have not made suggestions for radical reforms and are not likely to do so.

May I suggest however that it might be useful to convene a conference of American and other Non-governmental Organizations, particularly from the Soviet Union and nonaligned nations, to consider the problem of what can be done to make the United Nations more effective.

Paul Szasz: The past few interventions give rise to various problems. The nonaligned movement is a by product of the polarization between East and West. If that polarization should disappear then the nonaligned movement loses its rationale. They have an alterego in the Group of 77, which represents the South in the North South configuration. That is being preserved.

Regarding the participation of Non-governmental Organizations I have some doubts. Non-governmental Organizations have been particularly valuable in respect of technical operations such as environmental problems, human rights and to some extent disarmament and some other fields. But I doubt if they can really make a useful systematic contribution regarding the Charter other than generating ideas which could then be taken up by the real participants. Remember that they are, to large extent, self-selected interest groups, some good and some bad. Some overlap, so it is not really a tool for democratic participation.

I would like to suggest that the term "undemocratic" is not really meaningful when you talk about the structure of the world community as it is or as it conceivably will be. Nothing is democratic about the General Assembly. The idea of one-nation-one-vote sounds fair but that means that China with over a billion people has the same vote as Vanuatu with something like 60,000. The United States Supreme Court has declared that votes based on areas only is not democratic because trees and fields don't count; only people should be counted. Presumably the same principle could apply to the Charter. We are not talking about democracy in the real sense of the word, but about how the world can effectively be governed.

Prof. Rais A. Touzmohammad: May I comment on the observation that the nonaligned movement should disappear because the polarization between the blocs is disappearing? The basic idea behind the nonaligned movement was independence of the blocs and primarily economic independence. Even if the blocs disappear it is predictable that there will still be economic inequality and reason for the nonaligned to continue.

I would also like to comment that democracy in the pure sense will never exist, but when I spoke about democratization of the legal system with reference to the General Assembly I had in mind that it was a body which had no authority to reach binding decisions but was only a forum for recommendations. The Security Council, on the other hand, can act decisively and the need for democracy is greater.

Paul Szasz: I was trying to convey the thought that the use of the term "democratic" was meaningless in discussing United Nations institutions. At the United States Constitutional Convention the problem created by having states of different sizes and populations was dealt with by a compromise. In the world community the problems are of much greater magnitude in size, population, economics and development. A compromise formula would have to take account of those sorts of distinctions. I'm not convinced that any radical change in the Charter will find a much better formula for the present state of the world. There may be all sorts of changes in the world. States may break up or there may be greater regional coalitions to replace the present sovereign states. But as things stand now, the United Nations seems to have basically the right idea.

As for a new Dumbarton Oaks conference, I don't know if that is timely. A great deal of work would have to be done to decide who is to be represented and how. At this point there is no advantage in having the existing states as such hold such a conference. Non-governmental Organizations might add some new dimension. At the moment the people can only be represented through states. I don't see how they could be represented directly without first having a conference to decide that question. We can't skip that step. Re-doing the Charter drastically is not the most urgent concern of the world now. Basically, chipping away at sovereignty slowly, eroding it, is the way to go for the present. When it has been so far eroded that one can no longer speak sensibly about sovereign states, then it might be timely to consider a radical redrafting of the Charter or it may be unnecessary by then. I prefer evolutionary rather than revolutionary changes of institutions.

Prof. Benjamin B. Ferencz: Thank you very much Paul. I do appreciate the more realistic approach that you bring to our discussions.

Sandra Bendfeldt: Basically I am in agreement with a more conservative approach. It might be counterproductive at this time to seek a radical restructuring via a new Dumbarton Oaks. When, however, you speak of keeping Non-governmental Organizations on the periphery it sounds like adhering to the status quo rather than something which could lead to the objectives you are hoping to achieve that states will somehow or other give up sovereignty. The only way they will do that is if pressure groups, like non-governmental organizations, are given a greater status so that they become more influential. At this point I think it is in the Non-governmental Organization's interest to try to maintain a stable environment as it is in the state's interest too. If they can move away from the periphery, they can become a moving force in bringing about the change which we all foresee.

Prof. Benjamin B. Ferencz: I think the essence of what you are saying is that slow may be good. But too slow may be too late. When Paul began to talk about the United States Constitutional Convention I thought he would mention that the delegates were sent to Philadelphia merely to amend the Articles of Confederation of 1777 to make them more workable. The Articles did not provide for a legislature or for courts and it was quite chaotic. The same discussion must have taken place then as we are having now; some were saying "Do we really have to change it" and others were saying "No, No, let's just amend it a little bit. We won't give up our sovereignty." When they got to Philadelphia and began to work on it they found they couldn't just amend it. They had to do a drastic restructuring to cope with the problems of fair representation which Paul mentioned.

There are such proposals now being made by various groups. One is by Richard Hudson of the Center for War/Peace Studies who will join us later. He suggests a "Binding Triad" whereby the General Assembly could be changed into a legislative body by providing a fairer system of voting. We can go into that when he joins us. It is absolutely correct that you cannot move quickly on changes like this; they must come gradually and be acceptable if the changes are to be peaceful. The time may come, as it did with regard to the American Constitution, when those wise states-men who were entrusted with the job of amending it said that it couldn't be made workable that way. They had to propose something more radical and then it took another ten years for the states to ratify it. The difficulties that have been pointed to are all real, and it is correct that they should be put on the table. But difficulties are there to be solved and not to be seen as insurmountable obstacles.

Changing International Law to Meet Changing Times

Professor Benjamin B. Ferencz: Let me move on to more difficulties. Let us deal with a question of international *law*. What can we as lawyers do to change or clarify the law? Let us take perhaps the most difficult problem. We have seen from recent history that nations still commit aggression in the name of self defense, and aggression has not been deterred despite the consensus definition of aggression and despite the Charter's prohibitions against the use of force. How do we clarify the distinctions between the United Nations Charter provisions prohibiting the use of force and the provisions allowing self defense.

Dr. Galina Shinkaretskaya: When I studied these problems of non-use of force, self defense and terrorism, I found that they had much in common. One of the difficulties related to defining the offense. I concluded that there were things which could not be defined, such as aggression or terrorism. Let me put a pragmatic question. Wouldn't it be simpler to ignore definitions but try to find a way to regulate the problems legally? The Conventions against hijacking and other acts of terrorism are useful. Recently, for example, two Soviet citizens, one age 17 and the other age 20, hijacked a Soviet passenger airplane to Finland. The Convention against Hijacking helped to save the innocent passengers and to bring the defendants to trial before the courts of Sweden and the Soviet Union. Maybe it's better to try to work out more effective pragmatic steps than trying to improve definitions.

Paul Szasz: I don't see any point in trying to define self defense or aggression any further than they have already been defined. I doubt if the 40 year effort to define aggression has been particularly profitable. What is necessary are some organs that can reach binding decisions on the subject either political bodies like the Security Council or judicial organs like the International Court of Justice. These agencies should be entitled to function in that area.

In most instances, the Security Council was unable to find that aggression had occurred because the cold war split between East and West blocked their ability to reach decisions. If that disappears or becomes less important, and if no other inhibiting developments occur, the Security Council will be more able to fulfill its functions in that area. Furthermore, I'm not sure, as I indicated, that the veto power has to be preserved where the Council is simply declaring whether aggression has taken place or not. It certainly has to be preserved with regard to taking any [enforcement] action about it.

Under Art. 36 of the Charter, the Security Council could require states to refer disputes to the International Court of Justice for a binding decision. The International Court of Justice could then determine whether the specific action constituted aggression or a permitted act of self defense. After a number of such decisions were rendered, one would have developed a practical framework for fleshing out those terms in a clearer way.

Prof. Benjamin B. Ferencz: When I was a Prosecutor at Nuremberg, we declared aggression and genocide to be international crimes. The international community and the United Nations approved of the Nuremberg principles. But a criminal statute requires very specific terms. You cannot condemn someone for violating vague principles. It may very well be that you need a gradual approach of interpreting a vague principle over a number of years before its meaning is clarified. This was the case, for example, with the United States Supreme Court interpreting the idea of "due process. " It's a possibility.

Let us address another difficulty. Let us consider terrorism, for example. There are some who feel as I do that throwing a bomb into a school bus full of children is a terroristic act that should be criminally punishable under all circumstances. They would say that no matter how noble it may be to fight for self-determination or freedom from alien domination or for God or country or whatever, you simply cannot throw a bomb into a busload of children because that is an inhuman act which society cannot tolerate. It may be argued, in opposition, however, that throwing a bomb into a bus and killing 50 children is no more illegal than dropping an atomic bomb on a city and killing all the children in all the buses and killing everybody else. How can you insist that one is illegal and not the other? As we face the reality of the world in which we live, how do we respond to that as lawyers?

Are we prepared to say, as Galina does, that anybody who hijacks an airplane is a "naughty boy" and leave it to the courts to deal with him and decide what to do about it, or do we say that killing people indiscriminately, no matter how noble the motive, is prohibited - as we did in the rules of warfare (which are usually ignored in the nuclear age) or do we say that it's too complicated and too difficult to specify and simply affirm that everybody is supposed to be human and behave in a human way and then leave it to the courts to decide if the law has been violated. What is our duty as lawyers? Let's all go over the alternatives.

Prof. Rais A. Touzmohammad: For six years I served on the United Nations committee dealing with the Declaration on Friendly Relations among states. We codified certain principles of *jus cogens*. Non-use of force is one of such basic principles of international law which cannot be violated. The principle of self-determination is the same. That implies that one may also use armed resistance to attain it and states are obliged to assist. If a basic principle is violated, shall one just say that it is forbidden and have no right of defense? Article 51 (authorizing self defense) is widely used as a pretext by aggressors. If you are assaulted you must have the right to respond and we must have legal mechanisms to help the assaulted party protect itself. We have the Security Council. But neither my country in invading Afghanistan nor the United States in Grenada informed the Security Council.

Prof. Benjamin B. Ferencz: You are suggesting that as long as organizational help is not available, self help is unavoidable and also necessary. But if self help is abused and is dangerous, isn't it all the more necessary to create more effective organizational help? Art. 51 refers to self defense only against an *armed attack* and only for a temporary period until the Security Council can intervene. It is thus trying to curb selfhelp by nations which has led and continues to lead to abuses by nations.

If we eliminate the capacity for armed attack by putting effective controls on arms which can be used for aggressive purposes, (e. g by a system of "defensive defense, " which we may discuss later) don't we make it possible for more effective organization of some kind (United Nations, an international security force or court with binding authority) to reduce the risk of self help which is so dangerous for our society?

Paul Szasz: Basically, Art. 51 contains all of the essential elements. It defines self defense as an *inherent right*. Every organ has such a right; people have it and even though there are police forces there are situations where a person is attacked and the police is not immediately in sight. There are certain things you can and cannot do in exercising that right. For example, in the United States you do not have to retreat if you are attacked in your own home. In other circumstances you may have to retreat if you can. There are various rules.

Similarly, internationally one has to develop rules of that sort. The right of the community to help the individual also exists in the United Nations Charter. If the Security Council is effective in curbing an aggressor, then the right of self defense isn't eliminated but is limited. It is a temporary right until the Security Council can cut in. Thus the Charter says all that can be said. As Galina has pointed out, more definitions don't help in this field. What we need is an effective Security Council which can declare that certain action is aggression or self defense and, if possible, mobilize the world community effectively to stop the wrong action.

Prof. Benjamin B. Ferencz: The Charter plan also envisaged the use of an international military force, if necessary, to enforce Security Council decisions. That has become a dead letter. The Charter itself has not been implemented. Rais would you like to comment?

Prof. Rais A. Touzmohammad: The main problem is one of politics; in relations between the superpowers. Now that a certain turning point has arrived in the history of the United Nations, that may change. We are talking about the law of peace for the coming century. We hope that we will see the dissolution of blocs, a system of disarmament etc. Our current understanding of the term "force" is obsolete. Aggression as the use of military force is meaningless and will be more so in the future. We must consider other worldwide uses of different kinds of force pursuant to the Charter.

Dr. Galina Shinkaretskaya: Everything is changing now. For example, with regard to self-determination, we Soviets are concentrating now on internal progress and the Russian Republic (which contains about 100 different national groups) has declared its independence. But what does such independence mean? This is an expression that the people of Russia wish self-determination. But is this a right to struggle against suppression or against the colonialists? No, not at all. We are tired of being treated as colonies. We want to declare ourselves independent from the

Soviet Union. This is going to be a new state which is going to make new policies which must not be colonialist.

Prof. Benjamin B. Ferencz: If what you refer to as colonialism may lead to the tearing apart of existing unions such as the Soviet Union, does that lead to a more peaceful world or do we again have to look for some kind of federation or confederation or United States of the world in order to have peace?

By way of summation: We have explored the great difficulties we face in many areas. But we are here not merely to point out the problems but to solve them. Are we going to say that human minds are incapable of re-solving the problems because they are difficult or are we going to do the best we can with our minds and offer them for consideration? That's what I think our goals should be when we resume our discussion.

Enforcing International Law: United Nations Peacekeeping

Prof. Benjamin B. Ferencz: Let us move away from considering the strengthening of LAW and deal with methods of ENFORCEMENT.

Paul Szasz: You seem to have suggested that the Charter provisions dealing with the establishment of a United Nations military force are dead. Let's first consider what those provisions are. The Charter didn't really foresee a United Nations military. What it foresaw was national military forces that would be held in readiness. The most you can say is that these provisions have been moribund during the past 45 years.

The reason which caused the Security Council to be disabled in many ways during those years was because of the East West confrontation between states that had the veto power. That confrontation seems to be fading which means that everything that was put into abeyance during that period potentially can now be revived. There is no reason to declare these provisions dead.

It should be noted that particularly during the past 20 years the United Nations has developed a system of peacekeeping. It is in many ways as foreseen by the Charter except that it is a fully consensual system. It does not apply in situations where any party to the conflict has to be coerced into accepting United Nations troops. They must all agree upon the usually limited objective. The Charter foresaw the possibility of imposing on unwilling states. The use of military forces by the United Nations, particularly during the last few years, has come about, for example in the Iran-Iraq conflict, in Afghanistan, in the evacuation of Angola, Namibia and in Central America. You can hardly say that the process is dead.

Prof. Benjamin B. Ferencz: Of course you are right. When I said the peacekeeping provisions were a dead letter I simply meant that the United Nations force as originally envisaged had never been put into effect. The only time anything resembling a United Nations force of national units was ever used was in Korea and that was under special circumstances. Let me ask you, however, whether the United Nations peacekeeping forces as they are evolving by being interjected into various areas (and that is such a useful role that they earned a Nobel peace prize for it) whether that presents an opportunity to expand it further in the same direction, particularly in a disarmed world which would be part of the new configuration? Could this type of international military force drawn from various nations grow into a useful instrumentality to maintain the peace even if the parties didn't consent?

Paul Szasz: I think it could. With the relaxation of the cold war there is more and more a possibility of the Security Council reaching decisions which don't necessarily require the consensus of all the states concerned. The habit of seeking the consent of all parties to the conflict came from the cold war spirit. If that is no longer true, it may be that for modest, and eventually for more serious situations, United Nations authorized forces may be used where one or more of the parties may not be happy to see that happen.

Prof. Rais A. Touzmohammad: I cannot predict in the foreseeable future what kind of United Nations military forces may be used to enforce decisions. Because of certain circumstances I don't think it's realizable. I think that in case there would be an international convention signed by the major powers stipulating that all signatories are bound to respect the decisions of the Security Council, then it may be possible. But there have been many cases where the United Nations was too weak to be able to do anything, and that may come again. For example, the Soviet invasion of Afghanistan, or the United States invasion of Grenada went unpunished. These are rule violations.

We must also keep in mind that there are real political situations that must be taken into account; whether nations are disarmed or not, there are all types of disparities, economical, technological, scientific and so on, which complicate matters. They must be taken into account or else the human rights declarations would be meaningless. Therefore it is necessary, particularly for the big powers, to agree in advance upon the mechanisms to cope with these matters. They must sign the obligation in addition to the Charter.

Dr. Galina Shinkaretskaya: I fully agree with Paul that the United Nations military forces were restrained by the cold war. I don't agree that United Nations forces can be used for enforcement. My experience within the framework of negotiating the Law of the Sea Treaty indicated that the coastal developing states tried to obtain authorization for such enforcement forces apart from the compulsory jurisdiction of an international tribunal. Some developing states wished to exclude military enforcement but the majority would not agree to that. Some rights cannot be subject to settlement by compulsory jurisdiction of the court.

From a pragmatic point of view I would not say that the idea of enforcement by expanded United Nations forces is appealing to my heart. The idea of world government is popular among some Soviet scholars but that does not include me. If we take military forces of the United Nations stepping forward on behalf of all of mankind on the planet and the United Nations being a sort of government for the planet we will then come again to the bureaucratic structure which I am sure cannot promote happiness and a sound existence for mankind.

Prof. Benjamin B. Ferencz: When you refer to some states dealing with the law of the sea problems being hesitant about accepting the use of United Nations force to settle disputes, I, being an optimist, hear that as a good sign. The Law of the Sea tribunal may be a better way. You doubt the utility of a type of world government because you fear a super-bureaucracy of the kind you have experienced in the Soviet Union of so many republics. You may have good reason for such fears.

Perhaps we can think of ways of structuring such a managing agency for this planet so that the danger is minimized or eliminated if possible. My book *Planethood* spoke of managing the planet in a rational way but from what you say I gather that you would prefer doing it on a minimal level to avoid having too big a bureaucracy. It should do no more than what is absolutely necessary for it to function adequately and safely as a planet. Building up the use of military force may not be the most effective way of doing that.

Paul Szasz: Rais suggested that the big powers should enter into another agreement to abide by Security Council decisions. My feeling is that all that is required is already said in the Charter and saying it once more does not add anything and possibly just confuses. I am suspicious of any agreements that merely restate existing obligations unless there is some particular reason mostly in terms of clarification or additional undertakings, but ones that merely reconfirm that states will not start wars and will abide by Security Council decisions are unnecessary.

Prof. Benjamin B. Ferencz: That amuses me. As you know Paul, the United Nations spends a great deal of time repeating the same resolutions they passed the year or years before, as if to say: "This time we mean it!" You may be quite right that it's a waste of time.

Paul Szasz: There's a difference between resolutions and agreements. Agreements are basically for one time; once it is included, states abide by that obligation. The same is true of dispositive resolutions, such as the one establishing the United Nations Environmental Program—you have to do it only once. The resolutions that are repeated year after year are typically political resolutions and unless they are repeated they lose their political force. If you condemn someone year after year for its behavior and you stop passing that resolutions that suggests there has been a change. The resolutions have no legal force by themselves and their political force is limited in time. That is the reason there is a habit to repeat them.

Prof. Benjamin B. Ferencz: You are saying that political resolutions have a silent last clause which says that it will self-destruct unless repeated in 12 months. Very well, but let us now talk about the draft code of crimes against the peace and security of mankind.

The Draft Code of Crimes Against Peace and Security

Prof. Benjamin B. Ferencz: This is a topic that relates to LAW as a means of maintaining peace. It was dealt with by the United Nations immediately after the Nuremberg trials, when special committees were appointed to draft the Nuremberg principles in connection with the codification of international criminal law. They are working on it to this very day.

It has been referred to the International Law Commission. It relates to what we have been talking about. Aggression would surely be included among those crimes. But we have a defective definition of aggression and the challenge is to improve it or ask whether we need a definition at all. Crimes against Humanity, another concept that came out of Nuremberg, is also included but what exactly does that mean? Apartheid has been condemned as a crime against humanity.

There are also new areas, as suggested by Rais, which were never dreamt of in 1954 when the first report on the draft code was submitted. That includes new crimes like international drug-trafficking, or violations of the environment, international pollution of the atmosphere which would cause many people in other countries to die. Are these topics which lawyers should and can address in a constructive way in order to clarify at least some minimum standards of permissible conduct among nations?

Dr. Galina Shinkaretskaya: I'd like to put another question. I wonder whether only individual persons can be prosecuted for some of these new crimes. Gross environmental damage may require more than one person, maybe a group of persons or even a state.

Prof. Benjamin B. Ferencz: We had that problem at Nuremberg. We concluded that acts are committed not by impersonal entities; they are committed by individuals who act on behalf of a state. Even a Head of state, like Hitler or Goering could be held responsible. You are right that such crimes cannot be committed by one individual. We developed the theory of conspiracy. A large group of people could become co-conspirators to commit a certain act. If they knew that the act was criminal then they would be held responsible for it. We had the principle of "accomplices". That came from normal criminal law where a person could be held liable even if he was not on the scene of the crime; the white collar criminal.

The possibility of holding a *state* liable relates only to monetary compensation or other compensation such as giving up territory. You can't put a state in prison. Going back to the Magna Carta, it was confirmed that a head of state was also subject to law. As lawyers we try to impose liability if law is breached. Criminal responsibility for acts which are clearly prohibited should be a component of a rational legal order.

Gertrude Ferencz: I have a question in connection with environmental pollution. Supposing an industry is producing something and the by-product is damaging to the environment does that constitute criminal liability?

Prof. Benjamin B. Ferencz: That would be a problem to be considered in connection with codification; how far to extend liability. That also came up in connection with war crimes trials after World War II. One example was the case of General Yamashita of Japan, who was not present when his troops were committing crimes about which he knew nothing , yet he was executed because he *should* have known what they were doing. As a commander it was his responsibility. The principles which are to be expanded already exist if you want to use them as precedents.

Rais, you referred to economic crimes. Should such a code consider the wasting of resources by one nation when other nations are in desperate need? Should that be considered in connection with a criminal code of acts which threaten the peace and security of mankind.

New International Crimes

Prof. Rais A. Touzmohammad: In broader terms I think it is high time to codify the law that expresses the norms of international behavior as already contained in conventions and even customary practice. The Charter does not cover such things as apartheid and genocide which you mentioned. Things that perhaps are coming in the future are environmental or economic crimes. There are many of them and they are being worked on; books are being publicized about them in the Soviet Union and these ideas are being taught in the Soviet Union.

There are certain international economic crimes. There are several states and transnational corporations that are exploiting the wealth of other countries. This does damage to the people, not merely by taking profits but by damaging the lives of the people. The accident at Bhopal in India is an example. The same applies where big oil tankers leak oil at sea. The damage is done not merely to the adjacent countries but also to the people. These are not now considered to be international crimes as such. There may be a need to codify such things and make them punishable offenses.

Prof. Benjamin B. Ferencz: Let me go back to some philosophical questions raised by Paul and Galina regarding the speed of change. Perhaps we as lawyers can recognize that such things *should* become international crimes in the more secure world we are seeking, but taking into account the need for evolutionary development and the need for stability in the world, should we limit the list of offenses to be included in a draft code of crimes to those which are already well established, such as aggression, crimes against humanity, genocide? Perhaps we could list the others as desirable goals to be included later when we have so clarified the norms that they are more generally accepted.

Paul Szasz: Although I indicated that some things should be changed slowly, such as the Charter, I don't think this is as area where one has to go slow. The idea of clarifying international crimes is, I think, an idea whose time has come. First of all let's see what is meant by creating international crimes. At this point it simply means that it is a crime that states agree will be either prosecuted by them or they will extradite. They will not permit a person who has been accused of one of the acts defined as a crime to go simply free without being put before a particular court.

We could carry the internationalization a bit further by creating an international criminal court and an international criminal prosecutorial system or a national system, there are various possibilities. Why is it useful, particularly for crimes against peace? As explained at Nuremberg, crimes are ultimately committed by an individual and if you can prevent individuals from committing crimes then crimes will not be committed by entities. I do think that it is useful for various purposes to include corporations; while you can't put them in prison, you can punish them financially. As to states, I think there it is different. I doubt if the criminal prosecution of states is a useful idea.

As to what crimes should be included, obviously one starts with the ones that are already established in international law. You have the ones that came out of Nuremberg, or London, such as genocide, and now mercenarism has ben defined as a crime. There are several others that have already received that status. If one wants to codify them into one instrument I see no objection, particularly if the international crime concept is to receive a more general operational definition. You can then add the environmental ones as Rais proposed. I think one should start there with the idea of civil liability for pollution and so on and be a bit cautious about trying to consider various behavior as criminal if it would not ordinarily be treated as criminal under domestic law. There could be severe financial penalties.

Where you draw the line between civil liability and crime is a movable one even in national jurisdictions. One should be careful not to be carried too far. The legislature would have to do that and presumably they would be cautious.

Dr. Galina Shinkaretskaya: With regard to environmental crimes, I'm not sure that the offense is really environmental. For example, in the Chernobyl disaster, was it environmental damage; yes it was. But who suffered from this? First it was human beings, then animals, then plants and all this. What should be the charge against the one to be prosecuted, what deed did he do in depriving human beings of their lives or health. This was not a crime against the environment. It was a crime against the life and well being of human beings.

I'd like to draw your attention to another side of this very disaster. Who was to be blamed? Of course the immediate perpetrators were the engineers or others who were on duty when the disaster happened. But there were also some people in the Academy of Sciences of the Soviet Union who knew 20 years ago that this type of reactor was no good and that it could lead to disaster. Nevertheless they allowed it.

Prof. Benjamin B. Ferencz: As Paul said, the perpetrator must be an individual who is guilty of the criminal negligence which caused the harm. If he did so with knowledge that the harm was likely to occur and failed to take the necessary steps to prevent the harm from occurring then he is criminally negligent just as a drunken driver is who drives a truck into an accident. We had that situation with the Valdez accident of the Exxon oil company in Alaska which poured that tremendous amount of oil into the sea. If the Captain of the ship was drunk in the hold when he should have been sober on the bridge that would be criminal negligence which caused the harm. Drafting an indictment would not present a big problem.

An International Criminal Court

Prof. Benjamin B. Ferencz: There are the broader problems of what acts are to be incorporated into a new code and how the offenses would be dealt with. Paul has suggested that there would be room for an international criminal court, following the Nuremberg precedent, to deal with such crimes. That leads us into the question of the use of courts generally to serve as an instrumentality for clarifying discrepancies or ambiguities in the law. Perhaps there could be different chambers to punish violators for criminal negligence. Other crimes like acts of state might require different treatment. Genocide is invariably committed with the knowledge and support of a state as an accessory. I was involved with that myself as a Prosecutor. Sometimes it was the soldier who fired the gun who was the defendant and sometimes it was his superior in Berlin who gave the order.

Let's deal with the problem of using courts to reinforce the laws that we have been talking about. We've discussed the difficulties in enacting laws which clarify or set forth minimum norms of behavior. I think we have all felt that there is a need for improvement in the present system. We have seen the difficulties in defining such laws. If you want to prosecute individuals you must have clear definitions of the offense. You cannot punish someone for a vague crime.

Codification goes hand in hand with a court. If you wish to condemn something in principle you can be vague, but if you want him to be punished in a court of law you must be precise or it would be an unfair trial and probably violate the human rights we are also trying to preserve. The whole thing is linked.

How do we go about building new legal institutions that will be more effective than the ones we have today?

Dr. Galina Shinkaretskaya: Of course we have to think about new mechanisms in this field. The International Law Association has a committee on international criminal law. They do not consider using an international criminal court to try persons who are usually covered by diplomatic immunity. But it should be quite possible to find a way to deal with diplomats who commit crimes. It would be a good step forward in my country if the courts were allowed to apply international law. That would enable them to reach issues which would be excluded under national legislation.

Paul Szasz: The time has come for international criminal courts but the question is whether its a fully international system. One could conceive of a system in which the prosecution and punishment is national so you wouldn't have to build international prisons.

One could also have a court which is internationalized entirely. We already have certain international courts to deal with certain civil rights of individuals for certain types of transactions or torts. The courts settle their respective rights and obligations. All of that deals with courts that deal with individuals and that does not require a real quantum leap in the existing state of the law. A third one would be the one Galina mentioned a court that would deal with diplomatic situations. There are more and more diplomats in the world and there is more and more friction between them and host states and there are more reasons why one may not wish to subject them to host state jurisdiction. In the United States, Federal officials are subject to Federal jurisdiction. On the same principle, international officials could be subject to international jurisdiction of international courts both civil and criminal.

Then comes the question of courts that would control states. We already have some, like the International Court of Justice. There is nothing per se wrong with the court except generally speaking states do not have to yield to its jurisdiction. A court is only useful if jurisdiction is compulsory. In some limited cases you have courts with limited compulsory jurisdiction. Some are limited geographically, like the Court of the European Community. Others have a narrow jurisdiction world wide, like some of the human rights courts. In such very limited situations one could, one hopes, proceed to create other international courts which might permit individuals to raise human rights claims, environmental claims and other claims against governments. These would be in effect administrative or civil procedures.

Dr. Galina Shinkaretskaya: As far as I know, enforcement of decisions of international courts is always national. Even if the case is between two states, as between Denmark and the Federal Republic of Germany, enforcement of any international law norm is always on the national level.

Paul Szasz: In suits between states, such as before the International Court of Justice, states either comply or not; there is no enforcement at all and there is no mechanisms whatsoever for it. I was talking about enforcement in a new kind of international criminal court where individuals would be subject to the jurisdiction and there I said that it could be semi-international in that the procedure could be international but the enforcement or punishment is kept in national hands.

Richard Duffee: I don't think very much generally of criminal courts on a national level and therefore I'm rather wary about setting up international courts related to national courts without examining the limitations of criminal courts nationally. In the United States the primary use of criminal courts is to deal with defendants who do not have the money to render tort recoveries. The criminal courts generally interject the state between the defendant and the plaintiff and the victim receives nothing. The perpetrator is injured but it does no good whatsoever for the victim so I'm wary of criminal courts as opposed to civil.

Prof. Rais A. Touzmohammad: I support the idea of establishing courts. In supporting the idea of the rule of law, we in the Soviet Union support that idea as proclaimed by Gorbachev. It's not the rule of law over the state but the state in which courts rule and determine the law.

Prof. Benjamin B. Ferencz: We have been discussing the possibilities of strengthening the law of peace and we have begun discussing an international criminal court to deal with clearly recognized international crimes such as aggression, crimes against humanity, and genocide as well as the possibility of dealing with new types of crimes such as environmental crimes or economic crimes. We had mentioned some of the difficulties in trying to develop the law in that direction.

One of the difficulties recently encountered was in connection with the attempt to create an international criminal court to deal with drug-traffickers. This was a resolution introduced by Trinidad and Tobago in the last session of the General Assembly and was discussed and debated by several nations in the Sixth Committee. The Caribbean states were all in favor of it because they have found that they were unable to cope with drug-traffickers who were more powerful than the state. Drug lords had been killing judges and the states called for help by creating an international court.

But even with a court of such limited jurisdiction, unfortunately, the United States was opposed. The opposition was lead by Myanmar. which was formerly known as Burma, the center for drug traffic in the world; the Burma Triangle for opium and cocaine. United States allies also opposed an international criminal court. The Soviet Union took a wait-and-see attitude as did China. The subject was referred to the International Law Commission which was a reasonable substitute for immediate burial. It could be considered in connection with the draft code of crimes against peace and security which is now being discussed by the International Law Commission. They are proceeding at a pace which will get them no place in about 20 years; blocked by the usual consensus requirement. I doubt if they will produce anything of substance.

I mention that as an illustration of the difficulties. But difficulties are there to be overcome. In many areas we are making progress.

Paul Szasz: I'd like to add a historical note. Trinidad and Tobago really wanted to introduce the word "general" criminal court. The Prime Minister was persuaded that the most saleable type would be one that deals with drug-trafficking. He was hoping thereby to attract United States' support.

Prof. Benjamin B. Ferencz: Thank you Paul, I know that Prime Minister Robinson was hoping for more and indeed they made reference to other crimes in their resolution. The feeling was to take a "salami approach" of one slice at a time, expecting that if the Assembly would not buy that narrow approach they wouldn't buy a broader one. It shows that there are also problems of technique in trying to work through the normal United Nations procedures. The prevailing existing bureaucracy is such that they do not wish to have any challenges to themselves because it might endanger their positions.

Prof. Rais A. Touzmohammad: The Soviet government is dealing with the problem of international criminal law. The Institute of State and Law of the Academy of Sciences is preparing a three-volume publication on it. I'm not sure they have been able to read the book on that subject by Cherif Bassiouni but on the scholarly level we are dealing with the topic positively. We think that it's necessary. The government, for political reasons, may have other views.

Prof. Benjamin B. Ferencz: I think that's a very useful contribution, Rais, because it reflects the fact that there are divergent interests for and against such a court. The United States' Senate has before it a bill for the creation of an international criminal court to deal with terrorism. It was introduced by United States Senator Specter who recently conducted a forum in the Senate to consider it. A similar bill has been introduced in the House of Representatives by Congressman Leach. So far the majority has not picked it up and moved it forward, but it has a number of sponsors in the government.

So we see that in the United States and the Soviet Union there are some who are for and some who are against. There are also those who are changing. The Soviet Union, for example, was opposed to *all* international courts as an infringement on their sovereignty. Their position was also based on fear. I remember the minutes of the meetings at the League of Nations when Mr. Litvinov, the Soviet Representative, asked how one could expect the Soviet Union to accept an international court of any kind when the Soviet Union was the only communist country in the world and it was opposed by the rest of the world. But the world has changed.

The Soviet Union itself is no longer communist, as originally conceived, and today most people of the world live under some form of socialism. The original argument is no longer valid. Mr. Gorbachev himself has recognized that and for the first time in history he has been talking about an international court and accepting international jurisdiction on some limited basis. At least they are moving.

Improving the International Court of Justice

Professor Benjamin B. Ferencz: That leads us to consider the International Court in the Hague which was set up by the United States.

Prof. Rais A. Touzmohammad: Correction—by the League of Nations!

Prof. Benjamin B. Ferencz: Of course it was set up by the League, but the moving party was the United States and it even paid for the building at the Hague. Galina interjects that it was really set up by the Soviet Union and that Andrew Carnegie, who paid for the building acted in a private capacity. Paul reminds us that it was not an international court at that time but only an arbitral tribunal. But leaving aside whatever chauvinistic arguments we might make, the important point is that what was once known as the world's most unused courthouse is now used. The International Court of Justice is as far as humankind has come so far in creating an international tribunal to deal with various international disputes. But it doesn't seem to work very well at times. Do you share that opinion and what do you think can be done about it?

Paul Szasz: As one who has been active in the International Court of Justice in several cases may I note that the court as such functions satisfactorily. Nothing in its functioning itself is the reason for the lack of submission of cases to it. It is true that because it has so few cases it has a very lengthy type of procedure and overly massive opinions. Because they had only one or two cases per year the judges got into the habit of writing textbooks on each case. A busier court like the Court of the European Communities cannot afford to do that.

What is unsatisfactory about the court is basically that states do not submit to its jurisdiction because they don't have to. This is true of all sorts of courts all over the world. If you have a court to which you only go voluntarily, most cases will not be submitted because at least one of the parties is likely to feel that its legal case is weak and will prefer not to have it adjudicated. The world community has not advanced so far that states can be forced to submit to the jurisdiction. If that were changed by changing the Charter of the United Nations then the International Court of Justice could become more active.

Another problem is that of enforcement. There is only limited enforcement although under Charter Art. 94 the Security Council may enforce the judgments of the Court. To my mind, enforcement is the least of the problems. Most states usually abide by their international legal obligations if they are clearly stated. For the rest, until the world community is much stronger compared to the overly strong sovereign states now, nothing can be done. For example, if the World Court condemns the United States for its conduct in Nicaragua there is no combination of forces in the world that can force the United States to comply. That's that and there is no use in crying over it. One should forget about the enforcement aspect but simply see to it that the court is enabled to decide more cases and then rely on various internal and external political pressures for the enforcement to be positive in most instances.

Dr. Galina Shinkaretskaya: In my opinion, the Court is not lacking in cases. There may be five cases pending at this time which is quite a large number. How do we explain its becoming more active in recent years?

The International Court of Justice was created by the western European countries based on the patterns of their own judicial systems. It worked for them and between them and maybe it was a real court similar to those in national legal systems. But in the changed world after the second world war when they tried to deal with new problems on the same legal structure the court turned out to be fully unsuccessful. It was really a failure.

The Court became more active and more successful after the Court changed not only its rules in 1972 and 1978 but also its own internal judicial practice. They interpreted several articles of the rules and even of the statute in a broader way. For example, with regard to the use of Chambers, they agreed that the parties might have a say in the membership of the Chamber. That was the practice in the Gulf of Maine dispute between the United States and Canada. It was a rare case where the Soviet Judge, Morosov filed a dissenting opinion.

The Court itself is changing, but let us look in which direction. It is taking into account more and more the wishes of the states participating in the proceedings. If this tendency continues, the International Court of Justice will be a device for strengthening states on the international plane.

We see that international judicial bodies are becoming more successful. Regional courts are beginning to work and regional judicial procedures are now being born. They are all inter-state and I'm not at all sure that it will be good for the future of mankind.

Let me say something which is contrary to what I said at the beginning. The International Court of Justice, when it was created was really a court of justice, a real judicial body working on the basis of law. What we see now as successful international courts are bodies which are not so strictly legal and which allow themselves to deviate from strict norms of international law. If our goal is to create international legal order which is strict and just and based on law, then I'm not at all sure that this type of international judicial body is so profitable for the future international order.

Prof. Rais A. Touzmohammad: I think the International Court of Justice is not bad as an instrument to deal with a kind of constitutional law in international relations. They could render advisory opinions without going through all of the procedures of a court and as such it would have a good future. There must be a certain division of labor such as international criminal courts and civil courts to create a sort of network of international courts and among them would be a court to interpret the law by way of advisory opinions.

Prof. Benjamin B. Ferencz: From what you have all said it seems we agree that the International Court has certain accomplishments and certain hopes for improvement by virtue of the changes in their rules and their movement toward chamber proceedings in which states may have a bigger say. Rais has pointed to new avenues in which the court could be effective by way of advisory opinions on questions of interpretation of law or constitutional questions which could be referred to the court by either the Secretary General of the United Nations or the General Assembly or some other body.

These are encouraging thoughts but we come back to Paul's basic observation that courts are really only useful if they have compulsory jurisdiction. That, unfortunately, doesn't exist. We also have some problem of enforcement. Although the Security Council may enforce decisions, it may depend upon the political climate and if they don't enforce the decisions we do not have any other mechanism under the present structure. He says there is no use crying about it but it seems to me that there is reason to cry if a court renders a judgment and the parties just walk away and ignore it. If they did that in domestic jurisdiction we'd have even more chaos than Richard Duffee describes.

I put the question to you as international lawyers: we are trying to create a lawful structure that is more effective than what we have today. The International Court of Justice has fallen into disrepute in many areas, largely because of the United States walking away in response to the Nicaragua decision against it.

Paul Szasz: Why should the Court fall in disrepute because the United States walks out?

Prof. Benjamin B. Ferencz: The reason it falls into disrepute is that it becomes clear that the court has no authority and no power. Let Galina comment and you can then elaborate on your point further Paul, if you wish.

Dr. Galina Shinkaretskaya: It depends on how you look at the enforcement problem. If you say that the United States said "bye-bye honey" to the International Court of Justice this does not mean that the decision of the court was ineffective. What was happening in Central America was condemned by the International Court of Justice. That situation has changed now because of the change of government in Nicaragua. In the long run we will see the same result as if the United States had obeyed the International Court of Justice order.

If we look at other decisions of the International Court of Justice which were not complied with we see that in every case the ultimate goals were accomplished in the long run. We see therefore that enforcement is achieved; even if we don't know where the force is coming from it's there. The United States left the International Court of Justice but nothing really changed in their legal connections to the Court. While they accepted article 36(2) in fact they didn't accept it because of the reservations which made the obligations meaningless. The obligation under Article 36(1) of the International Court of Justice statute to accept the court's jurisdiction regarding treaties remains in effect. Even after leaving the International Court of Justice, the United States submitted a new case regarding an Electronic company which was decided last year. What seems to be white on the surface changes on second glance to black. It's not that simple.

Paul Szasz: What you are referring to isn't really enforcement but compliance and I agree with what you said about that. Practically all International Court of Justice decisions have been complied with, even if it was not always immediate. Five or six cases before the court is a lot considering the court's own history but not compared to other courts, or to the number of disputes existing in the world that cry for judicial settlement.

The formation of International Court of Justice chambers is an improvement. Judge Morisov, with some justification, objected to the United States submission on the condition that the United States be consulted regarding the judges on the Chamber. In the Nicaragua case the jurisdiction was not killed because of the Connelly reservation because that was not raised. Judge Schwebel noted that the existence of the Connelly reservation meant that there was no submission whatsoever under Art.36(2) a point made by other states in other cases.

Prof. Benjamin B. Ferencz: Without getting too involved in the arguments pro and con regarding specific cases, I'd like to ask whether the International Court of Justice is now working so well that there is no need for improvement and no room for improvement.

Dr. Galina Shinkaretskaya: I think the Court is good for the time being. Our two countries have just invented a new method to use the court. In the meeting between (United States Secretary of State) Mr. Baker and Mr, Shevardnadze in Wyoming last year an agreement was reached to accept the compulsory jurisdiction of the International Court of Justice on specific categories of cases and within definite limits. No one said this was contrary to law. This was much better than appearing to accept the jurisdiction and then making reservations which restrict or eliminate the jurisdiction.

Paul Szasz: The trouble with that agreement is that it hasn't really been reached. It was conditional upon other members of the Security Council also agreeing. Since neither France nor China agreed to the jurisdiction of the International Court of Justice, an impossible condition precedent was set, which presumably the parties knew. It was optically a very nice agreement but actually it was quite meaningless.

Prof. Rais A. Touzmohammad: It would be much better if the two superpower could agree without the type of conditions which Paul mentioned. They should show an example to the rest of the world. Acceptance of such agreements should be unconditional, or as Paul interjects, it may not be useful at all.

Prof. Benjamin B. Ferencz: Perhaps it's useful as an optical indicator that states are, in principle, inclined to move in that direction. That would have some utility even though in substance you don't end up with much.

Dr. Galina Shinkaretskaya: Such "unconditional" acceptance of the jurisdiction of the International Court of Justice would be contrary to international law. International law obliges the subject of international relations to act *bona fide* in good faith. Everybody could say that the Soviet Union and the United States accepting that apparent unconditional jurisdiction would not have been acting *bona fide* because they are not really *ready* to accept such compulsory jurisdiction unconditionally.

Paul Szasz: There was never any talk of unconditional submission. The submission was to be very limited to certain types of agreements and treaties and so on. While there may not be any conditions other than the political one which is impossible to meet I don't think it would be *mala fides.*

Prof. Benjamin B. Ferencz: So we have three views: Galina says such an agreement which only *seems* to be an acceptance of the International Court of Justice is contrary to international law because it's done in bad faith. Paul thinks it's not useful but that doesn't make it bad faith. I point to some optical value of good intentions. The basic question remains: how can we improve the International Court of Justice?

Galina said the original Permanent Court of International Justice as created by the western states after World War I worked reasonably well. But in our new expanded society of 160 sovereign states, are the interests of the nonaligned or underdeveloped states which did not exist as states at that time adequately represented in the court itself, in the philosophy of the court, in its rules? The United Nations has just set up a fund to make it easier for poor states to appeal to the International Court of Justice but what I am asking is whether the International Court of Justice as now constituted is adequate to meet the new needs of the 21st century or does it call for revision?

Dr. Galina Shinkaretskaya: I object to your assumptions. You assume that the judges appointed to the court carry with them their national philosophies and legal perceptions but international judges are supposed to get rid of such national biases and be bound only by international law. The independence of judges is very important, whether he be African or Soviet he must be led only by international law and nothing else for the benefit of all mankind.

Prof. Benjamin B. Ferencz: That is prescribed in the Statute, but is he really?

Dr. Galina Shinkaretskaya: I know many American judges who voted against their own country's claim, for example Judge Schwebel.

Paul Szasz: It is true that all of us are conditioned by our background. That is the reason why the rules require judges from different backgrounds. To deal with Ben's point about whether the court can handle claims from Third World Countries it may be noted that now practically all of the litigants before the court are Third World countries. Changing the composition of the court may be possible but it doesn't seem to be absolutely necessary to attract Third World customers.

Prof. Rais A. Touzmohammad: In general I know that Third World country lawyers are not in favor of the International Court of Justice. Why? One of their arguments is that they were not present when the court was created and the Latin American countries for example, have different cultures and values and legal concepts and systems. Your question is relevant.

Prof. Benjamin B. Ferencz: But I don't think we can solve it now, particularly since our other colleagues seem reasonably satisfied with the way the International Court of Justice is functioning. I'd like to touch briefly some of the other new courts.

Other International Courts

Prof. Benjamin B. Ferencz: We have the emergence in our time of Human Rights Courts; specifically the Human Rights Court of the European Community in Strasbourg and the Court in Costa Rica for the Latin American states. Does anybody want to comment on whether we as lawyers see a need to do any improving to enhance peaceful world order or is it simply a matter of expanding their jurisdiction to other territories of this planet?

Paul Szasz: Basically that.

Prof. Benjamin B. Ferencz: An excellent two-word response. Galina says the same and Rais just nodded his head in agreement and that's even better. But you can't get away that easily. What about the Law of the Sea Tribunal which is a highly advanced evolution of tribunals to settle disputes covering an area which is much larger than the area of the earth perhaps three-fifths of this planet. Their procedures are now in the process of being worked out on the basis of past experience with other international tribunals. Galina, as one who has been dealing with it, are you optimistic about how it is going.

Dr. Galina Shinkaretskaya: Yes, I am.

Paul Szasz: It's a pity that we had to establish that court when the International Court of Justice was there and really able to handle that sort of jurisdiction either directly or through a specialized chamber. The entire gamut of the settlement of disputes of the Law of the Sea has many other aspects but I think as to the court they could have relied on the International Court of Justice.

Prof. Benjamin B. Ferencz: We have spoken about many specialized courts: an international criminal court, one for the law of the sea, for the European Communities for human rights courts. We see the evolution in a peaceful way of many tribunals. Whether they should have been combined or not is another question.

Paul Szasz: That depends upon the parties. If the parties are states then the International Court of Justice is appropriate. If the parties are individuals as in Human Rights complaints,or criminal matters, that's another matter.

Prof. Benjamin B. Ferencz: There are different ways of structuring courts to meet different needs but we see an evolving process in international society. It has not yet reached a point of clear formulation. There is talk about a tribunal to deal with water law, an outer-space tribunal to deal with problems that may arise in outer-space regarding the movement of satellites and the use or occupation of space and so on. Are these things which should be handled in a specialized way because of their specialized nature or should we try to move toward one or more tribunals to cope with these as well.

Paul Szasz: I can see no reason for a court on space as long as there is so little law on the subject. The International Court of Justice is perfectly capable of handling whatever disputes may arise. If there are company disputes, they can go to existing civil courts just as the case of two tankers colliding.

Dispute Settlement by Negotiation

Prof. Benjamin B. Ferencz: We are fortunate to have with us this morning Ms. Sandra Bendfeldt who has just returned from a one week study course at the Harvard Law School given by Prof. Roger Fischer on techniques for negotiation. This, of course, is very important in the peace field. I'm going to ask Sandra to give us a summary of what she learned so that we can all share her wisdom.

Sandra Bendfeldt: It was an honor to attend Roger Fisher's class at Harvard and I'm glad to share what I learned. His ideas are in his book "Getting to Yes." It deals with dispute resolution through a process which is designed to organize our thinking. Organized thinking leads to joint problem-solving and the fostering of good relationships. That is the key objective.

This can be done between any two parties, whether in a family or among nations at war. These processes aim at minimizing polarization. We don't have to trust each other or even like each other's ideas to establish a working relationship. The traditional methods of bargaining do not foster good relationships but often end with parties angrily leaving the room and refusing to talk. It leads to confrontation and ultimately to war.

There are tools that can be used in this process whether the actors are individuals representing themselves or acting for interest groups or nations. The suggested approach is a thinking tool that is explicit and universal; it is applicable to any issue. It is simple, easy and neutral; impartial and non-partisan. One must focus on the problem and not on the negotiators. The participants focus on each other not as opponents but as negotiating partners.

We must move away from bargaining solely to advance ones own position to move toward a balancing of interests. We need clear guidelines, or a map, leading toward problem solving. Fisher uses a number of Charts as a sort of map to illustrate the technique. If the problem can be placed on a diagram showing the reality of the situation in one section and the aspiration for changes in another, one can see more clearly in which direction the parties wish to move. For example, if the problem is disarmament in United States-Soviet relations, the symptom is that there are too many nuclear weapons. The preferred solution is a reduction. Recognizing that, the parties can try to create programs which will lead to the mutually desired result.

Fisher has evolved a 7 element program to facilitate the recommended approach to conflict resolution. (1) First you list the alternatives. (2) Next you analyze the interests of each party and list them on the chart. (3) Then list on the wall what your real options are and discuss them frankly with the adversary. This will offer new insights and perhaps open the way to agreement. Step 4 is legitimacy: what claims are really legitimate? The criteria of legitimacy must be the same for both sides. (5) is commitment. These are promises well crafted in areas where there is some possibility of agreement. (6) is Communications. Listening and understanding what your partner is saying is essential. Ask that it be repeated or clarified if it is unclear. (7) is Relationships. Some are more important than others but if there is to be repeated contact on the issue or other issues it can be very important.

If these categories are written on large papers on the wall the visual depiction of the points to be taken into account will help reach a satisfactory result. One must be able to see the point of view of the adversary and play devil's advocate.

Prof. Benjamin B. Ferencz: Thank you very much Sandra for that enlightening presentation. Negotiating techniques are so important that I wish everyone here would comment or put whatever questions they may have.

You have stressed the importance of fostering good relationships in any negotiating situation, and that, after all, is what this conference is all about. We have invited guests from the Soviet Union to join us as friends in discussing problems which affect our common planet; they are everybody's problems. We are, as you and Roger Fisher have advocated, becoming negotiating partners rather than adversaries in seeking the same just goals. Surely we all have a common interest in a common humanity. When one lists the various interests on a wall, as you suggest, it becomes clear that in many areas we share the same concerns and goals.

Inventing the necessary structures for a peaceful world requires an exchange of ideas and the type of dialogue epitomized by this conference. Let's begin applying here the principles made famous by Roger Fisher and his co-author William Urey about how we can be "Getting to Yes." We address each other not merely as representatives of organizations but as human beings with human needs for ourselves and our families and all other human beings. We look forward to a continuing relationship and to a process which will enable us to go forward until we all get to the "Yes" of a just and peaceful world.

Prof. Rais A. Touzmohammad: By "Communication" do you mean the clarification of the position of your opponent?

Sandra Bendfeldt: Yes, but with understanding of what they mean, and asking questions if you need to until it is clear.

Prof. Rais A. Touzmohammad: Regarding "Relationships" do you mean that the opponents have to try to understand the relationships of their positions or the subject of their conversation or something else?

Sandra Bendfeldt: Relationships can have many meanings but here it means good working relationships—becoming good working partners. They must become trustworthy by saying only what they mean and sticking to their agreements. One can be hard on the issues but soft on the people.

Prof. Rais A. Touzmohammad: As a first step should the parties sit at a table and start drafting something?

Sandra Bendfeldt: Yes, an element of the approach is to define what work is going to be involved on both sides. The issues are analyzed after being placed in a circle chart which shows the differences.

Dr. Galina Shinkaretskaya: I am really astonished because I was recently involved in teaching programs for young children and I saw the same elements being applied as pedagogical techniques. What's so amazing is that the same negotiating techniques can be applied in a wide range of situations from the class room to disputes between hostile nations. My first impression is that this is a very clever thing and very efficiently done; not only the presentation but the method.

I think the future lies with this method. This would sound most innovative to our statesmen with regard to their decisions in foreign policy. I approve it with all my heart. But we still have a long way to go in propagating the method and we should think of how that can best be done.

Prof. Rais A. Touzmohammad: I agree with Galina. Nowadays in the Soviet Union Foreign Ministry, instructed by Gorbachev, they are at this same position. There are various forces in the Soviet Union now digging out old ideas, old ideologists and authors who expressed similar views much before they were repressed or killed. There were many philosophers who argued for understanding the position of others. That's reflected in the French saying: "*tout comprendre...*" Understand and you will forgive. Now it's part of our diplomacy. We call it the principle of the "otherness" which requires an understanding of the other fellows position before deciding policy. That is the new Soviet principle on all levels of human relations and intergovernmental activity.

Prof. Benjamin B. Ferencz: Would you please clarify that a bit. You refer to the principle of "Otherness." Are you saying "*Tout comprendre c'est tout pardoner*" or does that signify "togetherness"?

Prof. Rais A. Touzmohammad: It's both. We must find togetherness, but it's so difficult if I insist on my interest only. We must first understand our adversary and that makes it easier to move, in the process of negotiation, toward the desired togetherness. The Stalinist approach was quite the opposite. Sandra interjected a quotation from Gorbachev who stressed that the main thing was to conduct affairs to reach a mutual balance of interests. That is the main method of conducting foreign affairs today.

Paul Szasz: I have some difficulty with such schematic approaches. It doesn't seem to recognize that negotiators generally speaking don't act for themselves but are instructed negotiators. One must distinguish their interests from that of their principals. For example, in a divorce action, the competing lawyers may have an interest in maintaining their own relationships in case of future dealings on other cases, whereas the parties may not care about any future relationships between themselves, and may instruct their attorneys accordingly.

On the world scene negotiators are in an even more difficult position. Political elements may control the negotiating process. Some "Hawks" for example may care nothing about maintaining relationship with the adversary or the negotiating partners. That's what makes it so difficult to follow a schematic chart. Academicians, as we are here, have no real conflict of interests and so it's easier.

Sandra Bendfeldt: I can answer that. Of course nothing is going to be easy or change overnight because of Roger Fisher's schematics, however, parts of the world have changed as a result of that and he has represented our government effectively in many areas of the world. Furthermore some of his students are from the army and they too are learning these techniques and using them. This is an evolutionary tactic and as it succeeds in one place or another its success will spread.

It may also be that even "Hawks" will at one point have to consider their best alternative to a negotiated agreement and it may be that taking into account public opinion may persuade them to take less than what they wanted. It is true that negotiators will always want to go back to their bosses and show that they did not give in to their adversaries, but if one considers that the alternative may be war, or in a divorce case that the parties may end up in court with increased expenses and an uncertain outcome, the consideration of the alternatives may encourage a compromise settlement.

Prof. Benjamin B. Ferencz: Another illustration is the current debate between the Defense Department which seeks additional funds for arms and a public which wants to cut the defense budget and use the savings for social purposes. It will be the same in the United States or the Soviet Union. Every military establishment is charged with defending against all possible enemies and will therefore argue that the other side is stronger and therefore the increased threat must be met by more money and arms.

But if the public has learned that increased expenditures are not in the common interest and communicates that point of view with sufficient clarity to those in power and confronts them with alternatives which are worse, such as loss of power, then they may accept an alternative as a lesser evil.

Richard Duffee: I am not clear about the difference between "Alternatives" and "Options", and why is "Communication" listed as number 6?

Sandra Bendfeldt: "Alternatives" means to find your best alternative to a negotiated agreement. That does not necessarily require knowledge of all of the options which covers the full range of possibilities some of which may not be attainable, and they are not really an alternative which you have. You are correct in your suggestion that the alternatives refers to what you can do if you do not have successful negotiations but options covers a broader range of conceivable possibilities.

"Communications" is intertwined with every dialogue and hence it is down on the list because the other ideas may have to be absorbed first before communications goes into effect regarding those listed above. It's really a system of active listening which has to be practiced by repeating questions and answers until the parties clearly understand what they are trying to say to each other.

Richard Duffee: It seems to me generally that one of the problems with achieving peace arises not from relationships between the opponents but between the political figures and their own internal competition. For example, after Mr. Reagan was shot in 1982, the most disturbing thing that happened was that [Secretary of State] Alexander Haig got up and said that he was in charge. The President was more worried about his relationship with his Secretary of State than he was about the Russians. Mr. Szasz was quite right in noting that negotiators have much more freedom between themselves than they have with their instructors and their clients.

Prof. Benjamin B. Ferencz: As usual, Paul brings us back to earth. If diplomats don't carry out their instructions they risk being fired and perhaps therefore they are the worst people to try to negotiate agreements. They lack the authority, but occasionally they have a "walk in the woods" where instructed delegates get together on a personal basis and reach understandings which they then communicate back to their governments and manage to persuade them to accept the new position.

Paul has also suggested something which reminds me of the arrogance of power, when people don't care. If they have the power they don't want to reach agreement because they don't have to. This is one of our big obstacles.

It is important to review negotiating techniques because that is the lawyers craft. Being a lawyer means that you are one who seeks to settle conflicts. It is not merely one who drags the clients to court and makes a big fee - although some lawyers think that's their main function and goal. The lawyer should seek to reconcile differences and that is the art of being a lawyer. To do that effectively all of the techniques discussed are employed whether we put them in a schematic form or not. I think it's useful to be able to put them on a wall and look at that and so we're grateful to Sandra and to Roger Fisher.

Sandra Bendfeldt: There can be soft bargaining and hard bargaining and the participants can still walk away with improved relationships if it's principled bargaining and not merely for a specific position. It depends largely on how you relate to people. Many Soviet delegates have been to Roger Fissher's course and are using his techniques.

Paul Szasz: Negotiators can indeed build good relationships by using certain techniques but in real life governments don't always buy the compromises suggested during a "walk in the woods." But to end on an optimistic note, it is true that if you are a good listener and really understand what is motivating the other party and what his interests are you can start thinking about such options which may lead to settlement. If you think only of your own interests you will not succeed.

Improving the United Nations General Assembly

Paul Szasz: Since we have already spoken about the Security Council and the International Court of Justice, I'd like to talk a bit about the General Assembly. I have indicated that I didn't think that any radical change was necessary in either the Council or the Court to be effective. I can't say the same thing about the General Assembly.

The General Assembly is an organ in which all nations of the United Nations are represented. Today there are 159, it may go a bit higher and may even go lower as divided nations which now appear separately are re-united such as Germany and Korea. For the most part the General Assembly's decisions are not binding on states. Certain decisions, particularly those which deal with the structure of the United Nations, are binding. The General Assembly can issue binding decisions on financial matters. By and large its political statements are recommendations only.

The other main characteristic of the General Assembly is that it works on a one-nation-one-vote basis. Some people say that is democratic but it is only democratic if you think that the sovereign state has a basic universal reality. Any system which gives an important decision making organ the same vote to a country like China with over a billion population and the United States with five trillion dollars of national income as it gives to Vanuatu with a 60,000 population and a fractional national income, is really not very sensible. You cannot expect important decisions to come out of a system which is so badly balanced.

That is the great fault in the system, and as long as it exists the General Assembly cannot rise above that limitation. Somehow that has to be remedied. How that can be done is not easy, and that's one reason why it's not being done. Another problems is: "How do you get from here to there?" It would have to be adopted by the present Assembly and it is unlikely that it would agree to drastic change.

Let us consider a change recommended by Richard Hudson in his "Binding Triad" plan, which I don't want to endorse but it has some imaginative ideas in it. Basically you give each state three different types of votes; one is simply the one-nation-one-vote based on membership; secondly

71

you give a vote based on population and third a vote based on the size of the contribution to the United Nations which is a measure of economic strength. Thus, the United States would received one vote in its capacity as a member, then it would receive a greater number of votes based on its population and then it would receive votes based on its contribution to the United Nations (assuming it pays its 25% share.) The Soviets would have the same vote as a state, nearly the same votes based on population and about half of the United States votes based on wealth as measured by United Nations contributions.

Let us consider for example an issue like the adoption of the budget, which requires a two-thirds vote. It's easy enough to get 2/3rds of 159 to accept it because that number can be made up of states that pay no more than 1 percent of the contribution from all states combined. They could out-vote the nations with large populations. The alternative would be to require at least a majority of the votes based on contribution and at least 30% of votes based on population. In an area like disarmament one might make the contribution factor less but the population factor more. It's a complex idea and not easy to reach agreement on it.

There are other factors that might be taken into account such as the Gross National Product (GNP), but that is harder to measure than contributions to the United Nations. Military strength is another factor that might be considered, but that is impossibly hard to measure (how to compare a nuclear submarine vs. 3 divisions?) and one shouldn't encourage states to increase their military in order to have a larger United Nations vote.

If you have an Assembly based on a voting system like the Binding Triad it can then take binding decisions and each state would be obliged to honor the decisions reached in many fields. Small states would in effect be giving up their present monopoly of power in the Assembly but in exchange they could get decisions which would also bind the big powers which today cannot be bound.

Even to make the Assembly meaningful in terms of political statements it is necessary to take that type of vote. Today the Assembly can make political statements that go against the grain of 90% of the population of the world, and 95% of the military power and 80% of the economic power. That makes no sense. It puts a premium on countries dividing. I once

72

asked Secretary of State Rusk to explain why the United States didn't veto the inclusion of so many small African states into the United Nations. They could have been offered temporary membership or associate or advisory or something like that. Rusk explained that at the time it was thought there would only be 3 large black African states, based on the former British, French and Belgian colonies. It didn't work out that way. By splitting up they got more votes in the Assembly.

Prof. Benjamin B. Ferencz: Should we as international lawyers recognize that the present system is not and cannot be legally effective and address it as a problem that has to be corrected? Either we intend this assembly of nations to be meaningful from a legal point of view or it will continue as a debating society which has not prevented war and therefore we must advocate change which will lead to a more rational world order.

Paul Szasz: I personally think it's necessary. Let me add one more illustration. When the United Nations was set up, there were 51 states and the particular distribution looked rational to the people then involved. Western Europe with 40 seats had about 20% of the votes, the Soviet Union had 3 seats, later 5, and Africa and Asia had 5 or 6 seats and that seemed to be about right. The United States had only 1 seat, but there were 20 Latin American votes and everyone knew the Latin Americans would vote with the United States, because they were in the United States pocket. That's how the United Nations functioned till around 1960. Then the entire system came apart as soon as all the African states came in and the Latin Americans politically broke loose from the United States. At that point the United States had no power in the Assembly except in combination with western Europe, and even then they didn't have a blocking minority. The new majority ran roughshod over the others. They adopted a whole batch of imaginative things like the Charter of Economic Rights and Duties of States which scared the United States and was entirely meaningless. It accomplished nothing for states like Mexico which sponsored it.

Then comes a turn with the recognition that there was no sense in passing resolutions which the big powers did not agree with. So they adopted a consensus principle. Now all important decisions are taken by consensus, including the budget. What does consensus mean? Basically it means that any state that wishes can block it. It is a big step backward to the League of Nations unanimity principle. But that's the only solution we have been able to find. Either we accept the majority principle which leads to meaningless majorities or you go back to what is in effect a unanimity principle.

There are some advantages to a consensus principle for it means long and tough negotiations often leading to an improved solution. But, at the same time, it takes a dreadfully long time to do and generally leads to the least common denominator of agreement; a more lower level than if you simply required instead of one negative vote say five negative votes to block it. You could require 90% in favor to pass the resolution. The optimum solution to my mind would be some new form of voting.

In the United States a similar problem was solved by the Continental Congress by the Virginia Compromise which provided for two houses of Congress, one elected by population and the other by states regardless of size. One could do something like that in the General Assembly; make one an assembly of nations, one an assembly of contributors and one an assembly of people based on population. If the latter were to be elected popularly so that say every 10 million people can elect one representative that would still lead to a House of about 500 delegates which would not be unreasonable. Miniature states would have to combine to get representation into that Assembly. That's one possibility.

Another possibility might be the one suggested by Richard Hudson which I have mentioned. The delegate is required to vote in three different capacities with different weighted votes. Some sort of weighted voting is necessary if the organization is to rise above its present level of importance.

Prof. Benjamin B. Ferencz: Not only does the present consensus system allow any single nation to block a resolution but, in order to reach agreement, what is produced is full of legal double-talk. Exculpatory clauses are written in so that the formulation will be acceptable to everybody. The clauses are so vague that everyone can interpret them as they see fit. To present such a document as a *legal* instrument, is, in my opinion, an insult to lawyers.

It seems that one of the things we could try to do would be to knock out such loopholes which make such instruments nearly meaningless. You have that in the definition of aggression, the prohibitions against terrorism and others. Can we as lawyers say that the Assembly as constituted is unfair and doesn't work and begin to consider proposals for improvement? Can we say that there are proposals A, B. C and D, that A has these advantages , these disadvantages and so on, and analyze it as a document so that the decision maker can clearly see the pros and cons along the lines touched upon by Paul? Is this a useful project for lawyers?

Prof. Rais A. Touzmohammad: It's an acute problem. But I would like to note the positive developments. Today, the five permanent members of the Security Council understand that there should be change. The consensus idea was itself a change and I think it was an achievement. In the conference of nonaligned organizations with which I am associated, all decisions are made by consensus. The nonaligned were the ones who installed the consensus principle in the United Nations. It was an interim accomplishment.

Should we look at the General Assembly as a body which should be able to legislate in international relations? When the United Nations was set up, it was not by chance that it was decided **not** to give the Assembly authority to make binding decisions. What was sought was a certain balance of power. I ask whether relations have sufficiently changed since then to justify considering a change in the legal nature of the General Assembly. I don't think that time has yet come.

But we should look forward in the 21st century to changes such as universal disarmament and other shifts affecting the balance of military and economic power that will make it possible to change the Assembly as well when the decision makers will face a different political situation. As lawyers we can make several suggestions, as Paul has done, but the decision makers at the United Nations today will not accept any of them. That's the problem.

If we learn to live with the consensus procedure and all of its difficulties in such a large organization of states, we may eventually be able to suggest something more fruitful.

Prof. Benjamin B. Ferencz: Do you believe that consensus is useful even though it produces ambiguous declarations which have no meaning?

Prof. Rais A. Touzmohammad: I was a member of the Special Committee working on the Declaration on Friendly Relations and I know how difficult it is. We, as representatives, act under instructions from the government which says that a certain principle must be accepted or not; it's a political decision. The result is, as you say, that certain statements are contradictory but it was necessary to reach consensus.

Prof. Benjamin B. Ferencz: If the political realities were to change so that the Heads of State were to say to lawyers that we had a free hand to work out something in the interest of mankind, not the interest of any one country, could we work out legal instruments that were not contradictory and would we welcome such instructions?

Dr. Galina Shinkaretskaya: The question deviates from the realities in the world today and from the duty of the lawyer. A lawyer has to take into account first and foremost the interests of his or her client. Even if I were given plenipotentiary power I could not reach a decision by myself without taking into account the interests of a particular state.

We cannot say that the General Assembly does not work. It does a lot of work in the pre-law stage of creating norms of international law. All of the resolutions, however legally non-binding they may be, help to form international law. They express the wishes and intentions of all the nations of the world. Here lies the value of the General Assembly. I don't think we should be so pessimistic in evaluating the Assembly.

Prof. Benjamin B. Ferencz: Suppose Mr. Gorbachev came to you and said: "I am your client and you must carry out my instructions. I am now convinced that in the interest of the Soviet Union and its citizens we should have a peaceful world; that requires binding and clear legal agreements on certain fundamental principles. I want you to draw up such agreements for me." Could you do it?

Dr. Galina Shinkaretskaya: I think I could.

Prof. Benjamin B. Ferencz: Would it contain a General Assembly structured as it is today?

Dr. Galina Shinkaretskaya: I would have to consult with the lawyers of other governments and take their interests into account.

Prof. Benjamin B. Ferencz: Good, you are following the negotiating technique which Sandra has set forth of seeking areas of common interest!

The nation state stands in the way of agreement because it is concerned with its own interests only and not with the interests of other inhabitants of the planet. If we as lawyers have the capacity and skill and awareness that it is really in the common interest to have a peaceful planet, isn't it our duty as lawyers to offer this to our clients? We must explain that the old system isn't working right and it's getting very dangerous and so we propose a changed system which will serve the clients own interest as well as other nations. Shouldn't we set that as a goal for international lawyers as a means of serving our clients and the common cause?

Dr. Galina Shinkaretskaya: However inventive I may be, I still like the system of the United Nations even as it is. Although I am liberal in my soul, I am a slow thinker and I think that changes in society must be taken slowly. The values at stake are too big to be changed quickly. True, fifty years have passed since the United Nations was formed but fifty years is nothing in the history of mankind.

Prof. Benjamin B. Ferencz: Can I ask you Rais, as a Soviet citizen, whether you share Galina's concern for stability and whether you think we should wait for significant change, perhaps until after the next war.

Prof. Rais A. Touzmohammad: I am not as pessimistic as you are about a third catastrophic war. If it comes it will not be because the United

77

Nations Charter is not improved. Does the hazard come from deficiencies in the Charter or because in the political field relations between the two major powers were so bad? And if I tell my client to follow a certain course but must also advise him that the case will be lost, will the client give me the case? State relations are much more conservative than personal relations. Why should we try to shake the complicated United Nations structure when, in reality, we have no constructive substitute that would be accepted? It works more or less.

Prof. Benjamin B. Ferencz: You have correctly described the reality of the situation but the decision makers have not been adequately educated to the needs. If the lawyer tells his state client that if you continue with the old instructions you run the risk of blowing up this world and I therefore suggest you change your instructions in the following ways...the prudent client will accept it. He may, of course, go to another lawyer and you lose your job, but hopefully you will be able to persuade him.

We have been seeking an efficient managing agency to deal with world problems. We have considered restructuring the United Nations as a first step in improving international law enforcement. We have dealt with the security problems and scanned the difficulties. In the social field, to end on an optimistic note, the Assembly has been very effective in creating many new instrumentalities which have helped move the world toward a more rational order. These special agencies of the United Nations have recognized that it is in the common interest to eliminate malaria, for example, and to deal with other international social problems. They have not yet recognized that it is in the common interest to deal with security problems in the same way. That is the challenge we face.

Arms Control

Prof. Benjamin B. Ferencz: Just as in domestic societies, if you are going to have a peaceful international society there must be control of arms lest there be unlimited warfare. Let us consider whether general disarmament coupled with verification is feasible. What does it take to build a legal system which makes it possible to enforce whatever international norms or laws are agreed upon by the international community.

Let's start by talking about one of the biggest stumbling blocks: verification. If you can't verify, what good are the agreements? There has been talk of a verification agency to deal not only with arms but also with verifying other accords. Let me call upon Paul Szasz to address the question:

Verification: Problems and Solutions

Paul Szasz: At this point there is one international arms verification agency in existence; that is the International Atomic Energy Agency (IAEA.) It's not an arms verification agency. It is for a somewhat different purpose. It is for keeping those nuclear materials and installations that are officially dedicated for peaceful purposes to remain peaceful and not be used for military purposes. Many of its techniques might be useful in an arms context.

The idea of international controls over international agreements is a somewhat new concept. Generally, they were not verified and it was assumed that states would comply. If they didn't, some other states would notice and appropriate corrective action would be taken.

There are many means of verification, such as espionage, satellites or other technical means of surveillance. International controls have been used in basically few areas. Some exist to deal with drugs and human rights but they may depend upon a state reporting system without an inspection system. Even the atomic energy control system depends largely upon self-reporting by states. But it does have inspectors and a system of inspection which has been negotiated in detail.

Some states, like the United States, have put very severe restrictions on the movement of inspectors. Every state is sensitive about foreigners moving around as part of a control function. Nevertheless, the USSR has accepted the principle of inspection by the Atomic Energy Agency and has called for other verification measures on arms control agreements. I think the time for international verification has come.

The question is do we want a generalized international verification agency? It could take over the function of the IAEA and deal with such things as agreements regarding biological and chemical weapons and other weapons of mass destruction and arms reduction agreements. The means used to verify will presumably be a combination of those used by the IAEA based on internal record keeping and reporting and on-site inspectors. Technological means of national control would also apply, such as satellites. The French introduced such an idea and it was studied by the Secretary General but both the United States and the USSR were rather unenthusiastic about it. It's also a very expensive proposition. Of course, the cost of a control agency is only a fraction of the cost of the armaments, so it would pay.

This is one field in which states are unlikely to agree to serious measures unless they can be sure that other countries are complying. Control by national agencies is not really practicable and control by international agencies is really called for, possibly with the inclusion of some challenging provisions by the nation states. If one state feels that something suspicious is going on, it can complain to the agency which will send inspectors to verify the situation.

In inspection systems you don't really expect that inspectors will detect violations since if there is a violation the inspectors will somehow be prevented from seeing it. Plausible excuses will be fabricated to prevent inspection. But most states are reluctant to be found violating international agreements and even if there is a slight chance of being apprehended, most states won't risk that. The very exclusion of inspectors is a giveaway that something crooked is going on.

At the same time that disarmament negotiations are going on it would be sensible to start negotiating about a verification regime and what rights

80

and obligations and budget it would have, and above all, what governmental controls. The governing or controlling body has to decide what happens next if there is a violation. If that agency is under the domination of the violating country or its friends, the system won't work. There is a political component. The agency must have a somewhat low trigger point to issuing disagreeable reports and if it doesn't have that it may not be trusted.

There are thus a number of questions to be settled in setting up such an agency and it is time for the international community to start addressing them.

Prof. Benjamin B. Ferencz: We are fortunate to live in a time when we have begun to disarm, including some nuclear disarmament, and we have set up a system to verify that such disarmament takes place. The INF (Intermediate-Range Nuclear Forces) Treaty is already in effect and nuclear weapons are being destroyed under effective bilateral controls between the Soviet Union and the United States. It involves complicated exchanges between supervisors from both countries over a considerable period of time. Both sides are mutually obliged to accept the same kinds of obligations and intrusions into their national systems to verify that the destruction of arms is taking place.

Can the INF Treaty serve as a model or prototype of what can be done? Can the new high-technical verification procedures, such as remote sensing which enables us to see what is going on all over this planet, make it simpler to accept an international verification agency?

Dr. Galina Shinkaretskaya: In the Soviet Union, verification is looked upon as a confidence building measure. Would anyone like to comment on that?

Paul Szasz: Yes, verification increases confidence and thus makes it possible to reach agreement on other things which might not be possible without such confidence.

81

Prof. Rais A. Touzmohammad: I also feel that a system of verification and controls is first a confidence building measure. At the same time, it is an instrument of enforcement. An independent agency can be used to enforce disarmament agreements but for other agreements, such as human rights agreements or to enforce other norms of international law, other modalities should also be considered. Take human rights agreements for example: The Optional Protocols to Human Rights Conventions brings in a right of individual complaint against human rights abuses. This is another measure of control.

There are many international treaties which provide not for supervision but for review after a number of years. This is another form of control. I am for the wider approach to the problem of control. If we look at various types of controls we may be able to work out a wider conception which may be applied to different aspects of the enforcement problem.

Prof. Benjamin B. Ferencz: It has also been suggested that one might establish at the United Nations, or elsewhere, a treaty-verification unit which would, on assignment, be the monitoring agency to verify that a particular treaty was being honored and to report to the public or the parties. The agency could deal with a host of subjects of significance, such as environment or security issues or economic issues of multilateral or planetary concern. That would be even broader than what you are describing. Should we have that in mind as we proceed down the road, or should we take a more moderate approach of going more slowly because the world is not yet ready and it might complicate our problems?

Prof. Rais A. Touzmohammad: I think we agree that such things must proceed on a step by step basis, with each step ready before it is taken. Eventually something like what we are discussing may be established. We have seen that many countries refused to accept such controls but, as time developed, they are now being accepted. The international Helsinki Committee is an example.

We should not look only to states to serve as verifying agencies. We must look to the people themselves and their non-governmental organizations. They must be given status under international law so that they can participate in any new international control or verification agencies.

Prof. Benjamin B. Ferencz: We have seen from this quick discussion that verification is a problem which exists in many areas. Different techniques have been evolved: reporting, inspection, a review process, on-site inspectors and persons who carry out the disarmament under the INF treaty, allowance for personal complaints, satellites, electronic surveillance and other techniques. Is it time for us as international lawyers to study all of these various enforcement and verification techniques to ascertain their strengths and weaknesses and then, based upon the knowledge derived, to be able to recommend which agencies or techniques are best to cope with different problems?

Paul Szasz: There are very few such agencies and it would not be too difficult to do the type of study you suggest. When you referred to bilateral verification it should be noted that they are easier to negotiate but are also less valuable since they give no assurances to parties outside the agreement. All verification measures have limitations. For example, satellites are non-intrusive but have no value for nuclear or chemical warfare safeguards which require that little bits of material be followed. You can see a truck leaving a warehouse but you can't see what's in it. Using non-governmental organizations is a valuable idea in the Human Rights field, but may have limitations elsewhere. I also wonder if even all disarmament controls should be combined into a single agency. It may be a good idea even though it may need some flexibility and adaptation.

To have a general treaty verification system seems to me to be going far too far. Most treaties don't require it. It's too big a bite to swallow at one time.

Arms Census and "Transparency"

Prof. Benjamin B. Ferencz: It was proposed by the French after the first World War that there be an international agency to take a census of the armaments of different nations. If you are talking of arms control and verification it would seem logical to ask: Who has got what? A verification agency would have to know the answer, otherwise what are they verifying. They must know what they are beginning with.

This idea was repeated after the second World War and was then dropped because there was no affirmative response. Nations obviously considered it too intrusive into their internal and security affairs. They felt that concealing what weapons they had gave them some advantage over the enemy. The logic is perhaps challengeable because if you think you are stronger it might be better to let the adversary know that you are stronger to deter him from attacking you. The difficulty is that you don't know whether the adversary is lying or not. If we could create some credible international mechanism to do an accounting of weapons its reports might remove some of the doubts.

In fact, because of remote sensing and other measures we already know a great deal about international arms and capabilities. Has the time then come for an independent agency to be responsible for making an inventory of the world's armaments?

Dr. Galina Shinkaretskaya: May I remind you of the words of Mr. Yeltsin when asked his view of communism. He replied: "This is a dream high in the sky." I truly subscribe to the idea of a multinational, independent and worldwide agency for sensing the military forces of states. It is a good dream but it's a dream.

I reach that conclusion because I know the reservations made by states regarding the jurisdiction of the International Court of Justice. If they would not allow the Court to intrude it is not likely that intrusion would be accepted to reveal what are even now secret military activities. The idea of protecting national vital interests is still alive, even though it may appear to be out of fashion at the moment.

Prof. Rais A. Touzmohammad: I don't think the dream is a nightmare. It is a good dream which we must strive to achieve. But I think it is too early to think realistically about creating such a body. Its an intrusion into state sovereignty. Before it can become a reality, disarmament must not only be proclaimed but must be much more advanced than it is today.

Prof. Benjamin B. Ferencz: What is not realistic today - and I agree that it is not realistic - may become reality tomorrow. When we have reduced armaments to a much lower level so that the risk to vital interests is not so great, there may be a greater inclination to allow the "transparency" about which nations are already talking. You must recognize it to be logical. If you are really going to have arms control you must know what arms you are talking about.

We are trying to create building blocks. There is a link between disarmament and verification. They go hand in hand. Until they are in place there is no inclination to accept anything. Until there are courts with binding authority why should nations disarm? Until there is a system of conflict resolution by peaceful means how can nations lay down their arms? If they are not able to disarm, what do they need a disarmament agency for? They must still rely on force as the method for settling disputes. You see, everything is linked.

These are the difficulties of which we are all aware. It is necessary to recognize that the solutions are not realistic now but we must also realize that they will have to become realistic. If we want to render a service to our governments and to our people and to our planet we must encourage the movement in that direction and as lawyers lay the framework for it.

Paul Szasz: I don't think that a disarmament verification agency is that much pie-in-the-sky. We already have part of it in place. For example, most states are parties to the non-proliferation treaty and are therefore subject to certain safeguards. The Soviet Union, which in the past opposed such measures has now invited various forms of verification. In the United States there is a strong movement in support of such measures - partly because they hope for a "peace dividend." Many people want disarmament, and will want verification and will be willing to tolerate the intrusiveness that goes with it.

Prof. Benjamin B. Ferencz: May I ask Rais whether the Soviet Union has adopted a new policy of unilateral disarmament so that verification is of no interest to them. They will disarm unilaterally, not to a point where there is a threat to their vital interests or security, because they now have an overcapacity to kill. They don't need to kill everybody twenty or forty times. It's enough to kill them once or twice although twice might also be difficult. As long as they have a capacity to defend themselves, why be concerned about verification?

Prof. Rais A. Touzmohammad: You are right to a degree but all of the unilateral measures of disarmament are accompanied by an invitation to other governments to observe and confirm that it is being done.

Prof. Benjamin B. Ferencz: Let us save for our next session our discussion of what constitutes adequate defense. If we can eliminate the arms race the verification issue may not be quite as important. I thank all of you for your valuable contribution, and particularly Paul Szasz who will have to leave us as we continue our discussions.

Additional Means of Making Arms Control Effective

Prof. Rais A. Touzmohammad: The INF treaty and perhaps the coming treaty on chemical weapons have provisions for the destruction of arms and an adequate inspection system. If disarmament continues in the future, as I hope it will, what is most important in the 21st century is to control not only the destruction of arms but to control production in a more comprehensive way than is proposed in the INF treaty. We must also have scholarly and technological means of verifying the arms construction process. Not only must the industrial production be controlled but the know-how must also be monitored.

We know that the nonaligned nations have been asking for access to technology and that in many cases it is used for military purposes. The problem of proliferation must not be limited to the production of nuclear arms and chemical arms but technological know-how that has military potential must also be controlled.

Prof. Benjamin B. Ferencz: You are quite right in noting that not merely *destruction*, but also the *production* of arms have to be considered as well as the capacity to produce. Jonathan Schell, who wrote the best-selling book *The Fate of the Earth* argued in a later book that we can't destroy our knowledge to destroy the earth but perhaps we could reach agreement that the productive capacity should be restricted so that at least there would be a cooling-off period before such destructive weapons would be on hand.

Prof. Rais A. Touzmohammad: There should also be restraints on the *invention* of such weapons.

Prof. Benjamin B. Ferencz: In our society today, the capacity of man to kill man is greater than ever envisaged in the history of mankind. The arms negotiations which are taking place at various levels are in response to the public fear and demand that something be done.

In Vienna, nations are negotiating the reduction of conventional forces; there are bilateral talks between the USSR and the United States, there are unilateral reductions taking place in the Soviet Union, there is the large United Nations Conference on Disarmament, another group deals with chemical weapons, another with bacteriological weapons - which they say they don't have.

It doesn't matter what you get killed with, in each case, you're dead. Even in World War II, both Rais and I, as former soldiers, know that the capacity to kill was enormous. It's a very serious problem; to say nothing about the enormous waste of assets, resources and talent which is invested in armaments at a time when the world is sadly in need of its resources to build a more peaceful and humane society.

Disarmament is a key problem of our time. But, as we have repeatedly noted, everything is linked. Nations will not disarm until they are sure that there's another way of setting their disputes. As our world is now organized, with independent sovereign states, killing each other is the ultimate way of resolving differences which cannot be reconciled by peaceful means. That seems to me to be madness. In the nuclear age it's a form of suicide. It is suicidal, genocidal and ecocidal and absolute madness.

Our problem as lawyers is to try to construct a society where we can go to the heads of states and the decision makers and say that what they are doing is criminal. We said at Nuremberg that aggression is an international crime and killing innocent people is a crime. Nuclear war is no longer feasible as a weapon. We must invent new means of resolving differences. When you disagree with your neighbor you don't go out and try to kill him. You turn to judicial means or negotiations or other peaceful means to resolve the conflict. Anything less than that is barbaric and stupid in the last analysis.

The various current arms negotiations, affecting land, sea and air forces, are going practically nowhere and are aimed only at lowering the level of capacity to kill from its present enormous overkill potential. Realistically, I know that this system will not be changed quickly. Nobody will give up this system until there is a better alternative in place to protect their vital interests. Let's start to build that system.

Defensive Defense

There has been serious thinking in search of a different military system. The Germans, who know what war and defeat means, may be the most advanced. German scholars have been writing about what they call "Defensive defense." Dietrich Fischer of Princeton and Pace, the author of *Preventing Nuclear War*, is a former Swiss national who has also been writing effectively along those lines as has Randall Forsberg, of the Institute for Defense and Disarmament Studies in Brookline, Massachusetts, Johann Galtung and many others. They have been studying the question of what is enough to defend a country. How do you do it without threatening your neighbor? When you threaten him, you encourage him or provoke him into an arms race in self-defense. But if he knows that he is safe and that what you are doing is merely to protect yourself without jeopardizing him, then he does not feel the necessity to arm.

A too simple example of the defensive defense idea might be the building of a deep ditch around your house like the medieval moat; you are safe from attack by your neighbor yet it poses no threat whatsoever to him. The Swiss, in fact, follow that principle. Their roads are built with spikes that can be raised to avert assault. Each Swiss citizen is a trained militiaman on call to come to the defense of his country if needed with small arms that pose no aggressive threat against foreign states. They could be secure without the need for an expensive military and yet they threatened no one.

Today, those who are working on the concept of defensive defense are asking : How many tanks does a nation really need to repel aggression, what types, what kinds of aircraft etc.? The process is under way and that is very valuable. Again, may I ask you as lawyers, what can we do to encourage that rational and logical process which is so less expensive and less dangerous than what we now have?

Dr. Galina Shinkaretskaya: It's not really a military question; it's a political one. It is the question of legal order in the world. One country will say that two tanks are enough and another will say that only a number of satellites are required. You could never convince the United states that the Strategic Defense Initiative (SDI) is not really a defensive weapon.

Nations can not be convinced to return to the technology of the previous century to defend themselves. Americans think that the more advanced the technology and production the more effective the defense will be. That is not a legal aspect or even a military aspect. I don't think it would be realistic to get together and promise to rely on antitank ditches or Chinese type walls.

Let us look at the reasons for waging war nowadays? Are we arming only for defense? As we review recent wars we see that they were not wars designed to conquer and retain territory. In most cases, wars were fought to restore public order which the intruding party thought was the right one. This was the case in Grenada and in Afghanistan or even in Vietnam and Korea. The real reason why armies are kept is that the governments of the countries concerned are afraid that the existing public order will be overturned or destroyed and replaced by something not desired or acceptable. Seen from this point of view, how can one speak of the adequacy of defensive defense?

Prof. Benjamin B. Ferencz: You have noted that it is difficult to determine whether a weapon is offensive or defensive. You challenge whether the SDI system proposed by President Reagan is merely a defensive shield as stated or whether it can be used as a launching platform for an attack. It is true that many states engaging in war argue that they do so merely to protect the public order. Would you agree that it would be useful and possible to lower the level of armaments?

Dr. Galina Shinkaretskaya: I do not think that this is possible. I am skeptical about that as well. It is not the level of armaments which counts but the military potential. That is a complex matter and is not dependent only on the number of tanks or other arms. It depends on the international situation. Even if you eliminated the weapons, highly educated people could reinvent them and recreate them or more destructive ones tomorrow.

Richard Duffee: I think what Galina is saying is that even if you conceived of a system of adequate defense that wouldn't bring you any closer to having that level of defense installed. If the purpose of the armies, at least those that have been causing trouble, is not defensive in the first place then formulating a policy for an adequate defense may be a good means of educating the public and the real needs but it would not necessarily bring about a change of policy. The first thing to ask is what is the real motivation behind having the kinds of armies that we have. If it's not defensive we should learn what the real purposes are and how those purposes can best be served or eliminated.

As far as the cold war between the United States and USSR is concerned, it seems to me that it had gone on so long that there was hardly anybody left who remembered what peace was like. That's what happened in the Peloponessian war. The culture becomes completely imbued with military and people don't know what peace is or how to achieve it. It's a military mindset that permeates their entire lives.

Prof. Benjamin B. Ferencz: I think that Gorbachev has moved us beyond Thucydides and the old feeling of enmity no longer exists today as you can see from our Soviet guests sitting with us as friends.

Richard Duffee: If the cold war is now over it's because of the actions of the USSR. They have been doing much more disarming and there has been no symmetry from the United States side. That tells me that the American military continues to have imperial ambitions toward third world countries. [That would imply that the United States military is not interested in defensive defence.]

Prof. Rais Touzmohammad: The idea of defensive defense has been considered within the Soviet Union for at least 15 years. There should be an obligation accepted by all countries or at least those which are influential militarily to subscribe to sufficient defense doctrines. At the last meeting of the Warsaw Pact nations, they already subscribed to the notion of adequate defense.

Those doctrines must also be subject to review. It must also be subject to international verification to be sure that the doctrine is adhered to. It must also be clear, as it has become clear in the Soviet Union if not in China, that defensive forces must never be used against the people. That must be part of the idea of defensive defense and included in it. No government should be allowed to use military force against ordinary people. Military know-how must also be brought under control in the framework of defensive defense.

Prof. Benjamin B. Ferencz: Could you clarify Rais, whether you make a distinction between using police forces and the army to suppress action by the people?

Prof. Rais A. Touzmohammad: We in the USSR have various types of military forces: of the army, the KGB, the Interior Ministry. Their roles are ambiguous. The army is used only for the security purposes of the country. The army is the army of the people and can not be used against the people. There are security forces which control frontiers.

Sandra Bendfeldt: When President Bush was asked recently why we still need NATO since the Warsaw Pact is falling apart, he repled that we need it to maintain stability in Europe. Does that mean destabilization of governments or support or suppression for various ethnic or religious forces in Europe? What powers are required by NATO?

Dr. Galina Shinkaretskaya: There is a non-governmental organization called Women for Mutual Security headed by the former wife of the Greek Prime Minister Papandreo. Women from 35 countries met in Brussels and we then approached every Ambassador of NATO countries and asked specific questions regarding peace.

We asked, as Sandra did, what is the purpose of NATO since the Warsaw Pact is nothing. Every one of them defended the necessity for keeping NATO. Some were quite anxious about having a unified Germany within NATO. I think it was the Belgian defense minister who argued for the need for NATO to maintain stability in Europe, not merely with regard to a unified Germany but also regarding the Soviet Union and other Eastern European countries. Because of the instability, one could not tell what such countries, and their generals, might decide to do. They might seek military action in order to impose martial law within their own countries to suppress their own people. Some felt that NATO forces should be maintained to absorb some of the overproduction in the western countries. It was stupid.

The McCloy-Zorin Agreement on Universal Disarmament

Prof. Benjamin B. Ferencz: In 1961, Mr. John McCloy, acting for President Kennedy, reached an agreement with Valery Zorin, Deputy Foreign Minister of the Soviet Union, for a comprehensive disarmament plan. It called for total, universal and complete disarmament under effective international controls. Nations could retain only the national forces required to maintain internal law and order.

It consisted of only 8 points that were basic: you disarm, you get an international agency to control all international arms which are needed to maintain international law and order and nations can only keep national arms to maintain national law and order. You create a new verification agency to make sure that the agreement is carried out. That was the essence of that very good, common sense agreement drawn up by a Wall Street lawyer together with a high Soviet official and accepted by consensus of the United Nations General Assembly. Nevertheless, it was never implemented and never pursued because of the cold war. I ask: Is it time to put that agreement back on the table, accepted in principle, though not in fact, and let us see if we can proceed with this today and make it real?

Dr. Galina Shinkaretskaya: I am skeptical about it. It was only a declaration and not a treaty. It would be like accepting compulsory jurisdiction of the International Court of Justice without reservations. It sounds sweet and looks sweet, but from the beginning the baby is born dead.

Prof. Benjamin B. Ferencz: You are correct; the baby was born dead. They didn't mean it in the United States and they didn't mean it in the Soviet Union. But must that remain dead forever? Can we not start now with a new baby?

Prof. Rais A. Touzmohammad: I am not skeptical. I think we may be ready to lay down certain principles or approaches to the problem.

Prof. Benjamin B. Ferencz: Perhaps we can build upon what was once accepted in principle and not lose hope. As lawyers we can still work out the modalities needed to assure the future of this planet.

The Enhanced Role of the Individual in International Law

Prof. Benjamin B. Ferencz: This morning we are going to have a summary of a book sent to us by one of our international law colleagues in Kiev. It is a book written in Russian by Prof. Evintov, who is expected to join us later, and it deals with the topic of world order. Prof. Rais Touzmohammad has kindly consented to give us the gist of the book so that it may form the basis for our discussion.

Prof. Rais A. Touzmohammad: The title of the book by Prof. Vladimir I. Evintov is *International Community and Legal Order*. The concept of the book can be seen from its table of contents. The Introduction, Chapter One is entitled International Community in Theory and Reality. Chapter Two deals with the Legal Order in the International Community. It considers the definitions and characteristics of the international legal order and the problems of establishing a legal community within the general principles of law. It considers human values as a basis for such an order. Chapter Three formulates the international legal position of states. It deals with the interests of states and considers those interests within a political as well as a legal framework.

Evintov also deals with western concepts concerning the subject. In my opinion he did a good job and summarized the vast literature on the subject. He discusses many of the right-wing American authors such as Rostow, Bryzinski, Richard Pipes, Schwarzenberger as well as such liberals as Schachter, Franck, and Friedman. Naturally, he cites the books of our much respected host Benjamin Ferencz, with whose concepts he seems to agree.

I think the most interesting point for us to consider is his concept of what the legal order is or should be in an international community. He feels that the core of interstate relations are the general legal relations between different subjects of the general community of states which are directed toward defending common interests and preserving values shared by all. He says that general law must be based on common values including cooperation and mutual exchanges between different cultural and legal systems. He sees a new democratic order of states in the future based on legal norms the substance of which reflect the balance of interests in a way consistent with all human interests. That is Evintov's thesis.

My own comment is that I am not fully in agreement with his definition that the international community as it exists today is composed of states represented by governments. Peoples are also subjects of international law and community and not merely states. The international legal order is the system of international standards of behavior as legally formalized by custom and treaty, but it encompasses not merely states but also individuals and peoples and their organizations. That's what it is now and what it should be in the future. International law is one of the most precious values of humanity. It is a human right which evolved over centuries.

Prof. Benjamin B. Ferencz: We very much appreciate your succinct summary. Please convey my appreciation to Prof,. Evintov and his colleagues at the Institute of State and Law in Kiev for their consideration in making this book available to us. Would anyone else like to comment on the book?

Dr. Galina Shinkaretskaya: We have to look at the reality. International law and legal order in the world are now being made by states and their representatives. The role of the state is supreme. One can hardly imagine entities other than states participating in legislation at the United Nations.

In my view, however, the world *is* changing. Non-governmental organizations are taking a greater part in international law making even though they do not actually participate in the elaboration of international law norms but they do act as a pressure group to move their governments in certain directions. I saw that, for example, in my own involvement with women's groups who approached the generals in NATO and made their views known even to war hawks. After getting answers to their questions, they went to Washington and approached Mr. Gorbachev and President Bush during the summit meeting and put forward their views on the future role of NATO and the Warsaw Pact.

In my country now the movement is very strong in the direction of enhancing the value of the individual. This is a long and deep-rooted process of humankind. The individual, the human being, is the most precious value in the world. We are now only at the beginning of this recognition. I don't know yet how it will be that every individual has his say in the organization of the world and the legal order. But it's coming, I'm sure.

Prof. Benjamin B. Ferencz: I'm very happy to hear that. Yesterday you spoke about the difference between reality and hope and spoke about dreams, beautiful dreams. We all realize that reality and dreams may still be far apart. I'm particularly impressed by your describing the human being as "the most precious value" in the world. Rais spoke of international law as being one of the "most precious values." Yet, the individual who should be served by international law finds that his rights are not yet enhanced. If the prime function of the international order is the preservation of shared common values, as Evintov says, of human beings everywhere, and we know that it doesn't exist today, despite the progress being made, what can we do as lawyers; what legal instruments, laws or institutions can we design to accelerate that progress?

Richard Duffee: As long as the veto remains in the Security Council and it is not possible to change the statute of the International Court of Justice to allow individuals to be subjects of international law, those nations with power will not yield it to the people. We have discussed means of improving those organs of the international community and must try to do so.

Prof. Rais A. Touzmohammad: As a result of the Stalinist period, the Soviet Union has been so far behind in respecting rights of the individuals that we continue to lag behind in implementing new policies. To change to a democratic system is not so easy. One has to consider the impact on such things as the economy.

I think we must look first to domestic reforms. There is a very close relationship between domestic law, foreign law and international law. Democracy starts from beneath both legally and psychologically. I think that international lawyers must unite with domestic lawyers to help them formulate common precepts. You, Prof. Ferencz, have used the domestic law analogy of law, courts and enforcement as the conceptual basis for a new international order, so you have recognized the connection between international requirements and national practices. You should agree therefore that we need closer connections. If we can achieve that, it will be reflected at the United Nations because the states we are living in will have to obey the people who agitate for change.

Prof. Benjamin B. Ferencz: We have just been joined by Prof. Nicholas Robinson, Professor of Environmental Law at Pace Law School and a Supervisor of the Pace Peace Center, who would like to comment.

Conference joined by:

Prof. Nicholas A. Robinson

Pace University School of Law, Expert on Environmental Law

Prof. Nicholas Robinson: I agree with Rais. I think that what we are seeing is that the international order of states is breaking apart. The nation state can no longer live as an economic unit; it is integrated into the world economy. It can no longer live as an isolated communications center; it depends upon integrated satellites. The control of information is truly that of the world village.

In the past, standards for human values, such as those of the International Labor Organization, had to go through states which served as a buffer and limited their direct application. Now we are seeing that individuals are in fact beginning to work directly with the international organizations through their status as non-governmental organizations. They participate in resolutions, in influencing delegations, in preparing drafts, such as the World Charter of Nature, with which I was involved, and which was ultimately adopted. The diplomats couldn't have done it on their own. The same is true for the Convention on the Rights of Children.

You can't make any of these standards real unless the individuals in each country want them to be real. The revolution of rising expectations and the new communications give rise to universally shared demands for better standards. It is very important that we strengthen the function of law and the rule of law. It must not be as it was during the Khrushchev and Brezhnev years that the rule of law is subordinate to the policy making of the communist party. That excluded participation of the broad society. We have tendencies like this in other countries where people try to change the law without a democratic decision-making process because the leadership would like to have it different.

We lawyers can strengthen the process by which law is made. A simple thing to do is to disseminate the laws so that people know what the law is. That has just started in the Soviet Union, but the tradition is not there. The Soviet press is now doing a great job on that. We lawyers must try to strengthen the ways in which the citizens can participate in the legal system. For example, the right of individuals to bring petitions to the United Nations Human Rights Commission is a way where the system of governments and people have found a place to meet. The European Court of Human Rights is very strong in that direction.

United States domestic law allows individuals to challenge government officials and even the Soviet Constitution has such provisions if the authorities are acting unlawfully. These areas must be strengthened.

Dr. Galina Shinkaretskaya: Just recently the Soviet Union passed a decree allowing an individual to go to the Court of Justice to complain about an official and even against decisions taken collectively. This was not possible in the past.

In answering Prof. Ferencz's inquiry about how we lawyers can promote individual rights, it's very difficult. We can formulate the ideas and draft them in decrees but we must first have the feelings in ourselves and to humanize real life must come first.

Prof. Benjamin B. Ferencz: Of course it's hard to do. If it wasn't hard it would have been done, and it hasn't been done. Rais has advised us to look first at the domestic scene because some societies are not prepared to consider the type of world order that Evintov wrote about. They may be too engrossed in other problems, whether it be seeking food or water or improving their own standard of living. The problem is how do we implement these new norms into the domestic legislation.

Prof. Robinson has noted progress in several areas that may be setting a pattern for us, for example the ILO which years ago formulated and put into effect minimum norms and standards for laborers. Most countries have made such standards part of their domestic legislation. Human rights declarations have also become part of domestic law. Thus law, and lawyers, have played an important role in articulating norms and in having them accepted locally despite the difficulties. The legal models are there for lawyers to take as a framework for new rights in the future.

Prof. Rais A. Touzmohammad: I want to again stress the role of non-governmental organizations in that process of bringing domestic law into line with the internationally declared human rights standards. The time is right for it. We had a large conference in Copenhagen to organize the non-governmental organizations and there will be another one in Moscow next year. It's a very difficult process since it challenges existing authority. You see with the current movements toward secession in the Soviet Union that the outcome is bad because it superceded the existing authorities. This is a struggle but lawyers should participate in it.

Prof. Benjamin B. Ferencz: I appreciae your candor in noting that within your own government there is this conflict between the bureaucracy and the demands of individuals and the hazards and challenges which it entails.

Sandra Bendfeldt: We all seem agreed that individuals, non-governmental organizations and lawyers can and should do something but we haven't made a commitment to doing something specific on which we in this room can all agree. We should list it as a specific subject for action.

Richard Duffee: The crucial impediment to human rights advancement is the traditional sovereignty of states and the fact that only states shall have standing in the International Court of Justice; witness the South West African cases. Contrast that with the success of human rights efforts in Europe. The conclusion that I come to is that human rights are successful on an international level to exactly the degree to which states are willing to yield their sovereignty.

Prof. Benjamin B. Ferencz: Can we undertake a commitment, as requested by Sandra, to persuade our governments to recognize that individual rights have to be expanded and given a similar foundation as has been created in the human rights courts of Europe?

Prof. Rais A. Touzmohammad: Our Association, The Association of Soviet Citizens Supporting Non-Alignment Human Concerns (SCSN), is planning to draft a declaration of human rights of all peoples and prepare it next spring. The Asian Pacific Law Association based in Seoul has a similar declaration, which will be considered in Delhi.

Prof. Benjamin B. Ferencz: I think that's a great contribution. If all international lawyers throughout the world begin to assert human rights as an entitlement of human beings, this right will be realized much sooner. Your actions reflect a continuing trend which deserves support.

We have all more or less agreed that there are certain basic human values that can be accepted as a desirable goal by all nations. We haven't defined all of them in precise terms but we have a feeling about what they are and we are making progress in areas that can serve as a model. We can undertake a commitment to further these rights as best we can as lawyers and if we do, we may reach a more peaceful world.

International Law and World Environmental Problems

Prof. Benjamin B. Ferencz: We are privileged to have with us Prof. Nicholas Robinson of the Pace University School of Law who is an outstanding authority on environmental law. I am going to ask him to enlighten us on the problems of environmental law, particularly as it relates to world order and a more peaceful and healthy society for all of us.

Prof. Nicholas Robinson: It's a great honor to participate in this conference. Environmental protection has become a major geopolitical question. It's also a major question of human rights. When Gorbachev addressed the United Nations General Assembly, he spoke of ecological security as one of high importance. The Assembly has decided to hold a conference in Brazil in 1992 on Environment and Development.

It's clear that we cannot sustain the level of economic development around the world without having a better system of environmental management. We have stressed the carrying capacity of the earth to the point where it is beginning to break down and causing harm to people. We must go back to examine how we deal with natural resources. Systems have to be put in place to better protect the earth.

From the point of view of international law, this is not very extraordinary. Certain basic duties are clear: the duty not to harm others (a specific principle in the Stockholm Declaration on the Human Environment adopted by the GA) as shown by the Corfu Channel case or the Trail Smelter Arbitration and other International Court of Justice decisions. Other states must be notified of potential harm and there is also a duty to consult to avoid the harm. The hard part is: how do you make this a reality? As Rais pointed out, domestic or municipal law is an absolute prerequisite.

In the Law of the Sea Treaty (Art. 208) there is a requirement for an environmental impact assessment in which specialists study the impact of a proposed action in order to avoid an adverse effect on the environment. That's probably good international law even though the Treaty is not yet effective.

65 nations have now adopted environmental laws domestically. The United States National Environmental Policy Act was adopted in 1969. It required environmental impact statements before any Federal agency could take any act that might adversely affect the environment. The State of New York has a similar rule. Canada has the same. I just returned from a conference attended by Soviet legal experts to deal with environmental assessments to protect the Bering Sea. We are all trying to put together a shared management regime in which such statements are basic tools.

The only way we are going to achieve international ecological security is by having strong national systems. There are two levels of such systems now in place around the world. The first level has basic pollution control laws, laws for parks and preserves and third, an impact assessment system. This level has been coming into place from the middle of this century. We find that despite that, in many states, the environment is still deteriorating. So a second level of laws has been adopted. These are now called "waste minimalization." The idea is to stop making pollution, to re-use by-products that create pollution and to avoid pollution in the first place.

We realize that habitat must be protected - the place where animals and plants and insects live is not restricted to parks. One must protect the entire range of habitat of the various species. Thus we have a migratory bird treaty and a polar bear treaty between the USSR and the United States and related countries. A comprehensive environmental impact assessment program goes far beyond these limited approaches.

If you compare the United States, USSR, European Community and developing countries you find different degrees of progress. The United States, for example, is still weak on assessments compared to Canada and others. The Soviet Union has very good statutes but only now are we seeing enforcement becoming more effective. Their park regimes have been very good. Their listing of endangered species has been a very good contribution. Their system of ecological expertise is improving and can become very effective because of their many fine scientists. The European Community is still largely in the area of pollution laws. Their nature sanctuaries are good and are beginning to deal with habitat and assessment.

The developing countries show a very mixed pattern. Very few have strong pollution laws. In fact, water pollution is in crisis. 40,000 children die in this world each day mostly in developing countries and mostly caused by water-borne diseases. Many have good national parks but there is little habitat protection as such. Many parks are in danger of being destroyed as the population grows. Some, like Indonesia and Thailand, have recognized that they need environmental impact assessments and give that priority.

Despite the emergence of these two stage approaches, the fact is that the system is failing. World environmental problems are growing faster than the means to protect against them. The United States continues to waste a great deal of its resources. Seven states have taken ground water which came from the glaciers and have so expended it that we have only 40 years of water left from that aquifer. After it's gone, we in the United States will have the problem which you in the Soviet Union have with the Aral Sea where there is no more water. No one is quite sure how we can solve this problem - despite many proposals.

We still have tremendous acid rain and only now is Congress passing corrective legislation. We have toxic air-pollutants which are only now being identified as toxic.

The biggest problems we face for the world as a whole are caused by the chloroflurocarbons (CFC) and refrigerants that continue to deplete the ozone layer despite the Montreal Protocol and other agreements. It will take us more than ten years to eliminate these substances and meanwhile skin cancer caused by the erosion of the ultraviolet ray shield of the stratospheric ozone will increase. The productivity of plankton in the oceans will decrease and the food chain including fish will be threatened. CFC molecules and carbon dioxide emissions caused by burning fossil fuels absorb sunlight and thereby cause the earth to be excessively warmed.

As the population grows rapidly in developing countries, it is estimated that another billion people will be added in the next decade. They will require agriculture which produces methane which is a greenhouse gas which may produce more such gases by that time than produced by in-

105

dustrial countries. Global warming is not just a rich country phenomenon. The problem is global. The heating up of the earth has caused shifts in climate patterns in different areas. We can, for example, no longer predict good rainfall in certain regions. We already have unpredictable storms and sealevel rises - with disastrous consequences to adjacent areas.

At the same time, in many areas we are cutting down our forests very rapidly. In the tropics we are probably killing off 20% of all species on the face of the earth today. These trends have been studied by the United Nations and its commissions such as the Brundtland Commission which concluded that the trends are proceeding faster than we can cope with them. The result was the recognition of the tremendous need for new international environmental law.

We cannot wait for every nation to come to the same conclusion on their own. We must all change our patterns quickly. Lawyers must start to harmonize the national legal systems. You can not have inconsistent standards as far as nature goes. The laws of nature are the same in the Soviet Union, in the United States and elsewhere. We must conform our human behavior to protect those natural systems. We can no longer be so proud as to say that we will change or control nature. We can work with nature and improve certain things a bit but we can not continue the pattern of the last century which destroys the natural systems that sustain us. If we don't, we will, like other endangered species, end up by destroying our own home.

This is an appropriate topic of international law. There are narrow questions where issues of dispute settlement and ecology come together, such as where countries threaten to cut off the flow of rivers to other nations. You have this regarding the Nile. In Canada, a flood control project would have affected the river systems in several states. Canadian citizens challenged the Canadian impact statement and won a decision requiring a more comprehensive study to include the impact in the United States. That's an example of the role of courts to implement international law. Assessment is basically a fact-finding technique by scientists.

Although we have seen the emergence of environmental protection as a top priority, my greatest fear is that the hazards are growing faster than our capacity to limit it. We have still not spent enough time on the problem. In the Soviet Union today there is a real dispute going on and it will be a real challenge to democracy to see if the Soviet bureaucracy will be willing to do all that is required. It will have its impact on the environment in the United States as well. We all share one biosphere and we are all affected. It's a slow process but we need to build up the environmental systems in many parts of the world to an international standard mutually defined.

Prof. Benjamin B. Ferencz: Thank you very much Prof. Robinson for that very excellent and comprehensive report. The picture that you place before us is one of a very endangered planet. Jonathan Schell, in his book *The Fate of the Earth*, warned that the danger of nuclear war threatened the total destruction of the earth. From your description, that danger exists even without a nuclear war if we don't make the necessary changes.

Your report of 40,000 children dying each *day* because of the absence of clean drinking water lays before us a new Holocaust of enormous dimension yet one which is almost totally ignored in the rest of the world. We as lawyers should be terrified if we can see this happen without being engaged in the process of trying to prevent it. It's part of the challenge of trying to create a peaceful world. Environment is a planetary problem. It's absurd to consider it a national problem only. It also ties in with the problem of social justice we must consider. How can one nation be polluting the environment to the endangerment of others while others are without water or food and other necessities for survival?

As lawyers, we can urge our governments and the United Nations to agree upon certain standards which require that the environment shall not be violated. With veto powers, consensus and other limitations, the United Nations is not likely to be effective enough. Existing international courts of various kinds do not normally deal with environmental problems. Perhaps they should.

Perhaps we should declare as a fundamental human right the right to breathe fresh air and drink clean water. Perhaps there should be a special international environmental court to deal with that. Should the Security Council be given authority to enforce environmental laws? These should not usually involve the same types of conflicts of interest that one has in military conflicts. A sound environment should be a matter of *common interest*. Should it be a crime for a head of state to violate the accepted standards? These are legal problems which we can and should address as lawyers. There are legal instrumentalities which are before us as models.

Should we agree that these are matters we wish to bring to the attention of our governments and agree that they are worthwhile objectives? Must we start to scream? Shall we use the communications capability now in the world to elicit broad support from the people, the non-governmental organizations and peoples of the world?

Prof. Rais A. Touzmohammad: My feeling is that we should help to move the process forward from both the national and the international levels. We've had a very bad history in the Soviet Union where lakes are poisoned by chemicals even though it was forbidden. I saw this is my own region of Uzbekistan. The government will only respond when it is forced to do so by the people. Intellectuals must explain what harm is being done to the people by such abuse. The government ministers can not break free from their bureaucratic system. The non-governmental organizations may have an important influence.

For example, our non-governmental organization association took the initiative to raise the problem of preserving the environment of the mountains - a new and important topic. That includes not merely water and habitation but also rocks. When I approached the government ministers in Khirgizia, where there are mountain ranges, they didn't understand why any protection was needed. We are planning a conference on it and would like to welcome as many foreign experts as we can to share their laws and experiences with us before it is too late.

Prof. Benjamin B. Ferencz: You have recognized that the people to whom you look for action are themselves unaware of the problem or they don't feel they have any real choices. Poor people who feel they must cut down the forest because they need the wood for fuel to heat their food may not know what else they can do. Let me put a question to Dr. Rose Cooper who has just joined us. She is not a lawyer but is an educator here at Pace University and she has been engaged in peace issues for a long time. As a concerned human being, do you have any thoughts about don't feel they have any real choices. Poor people who feel they must cut down the forest because they need the wood for fuel to heat their food may not know what else they can do. Let me put a question to Dr. Rose Cooper who has just joined us. She is not a lawyer but is an educator here at Pace University and she has been engaged in peace issues for a long time. As a concerned human being, do you have any thoughts about how to alert the public, upon whose support we must depend, to recognize this great environmental hazard which faces all human beings?

Dr. Rose Cooper: Our Guidance Association had an international conference in England last year which covered many multi-cultural issues. We felt as Counsellors that the only tool at our disposal was education by every possible means to make people aware of the problem and that the real power was in their own hands. We are not putting out the message about how serious the environmental problems are. Education crosses all national boundaries and we must use it more effectively to influence governments to appropriate action.

Conference joined by:

Dr. Rose Cooper
Educator, Pace University

Richard Duffee: I have found that dedicated individuals too often have to struggle for recognition or funds to be able to carry on their activities in the public interest. Taking legal action, which is often indicated, means they must have money for attorney's fees. There are legislative changes which are necessary to enable courageous citizens to recover attorney's fees and to encourage them to maintain their interest and be stimulated to seek more education on specific public issues. Very often they just get more frustrated.

Prof. Benjamin B. Ferencz: Of course, all of us are frustrated at times since we are, as Galina says, still among the dreamers in a world full of difficulties. That makes it all the more necessary for us to try harder. We can all agree that we have a common interest in a safe and healthy envi-

Dr. Galina Shinkaretskaya: Yes, I can agree with that. I suggest that we have an international body, like the Commission on Human Rights, to which states would have to report on what they are doing to protect the environment.

Prof. Benjamin B. Ferencz: That's an excellent idea. We might get a General Assembly resolution calling upon all states to issue annual reports dealing with all of the items referred to by Prof. Robinson as essential for the safety of mankind.

Prof. Rais A. Touzmohammad: I fully agree with Galina but we should not forget to include the non-governmental organizations on an equal footing with states.

Prof. Benjamin B. Ferencz: Of course, we spoke about democratic participation in all issues which affect all human beings. That is one of the things which we as lawyers will have to work out.

Visions of a World Federation of Peace and Justice

Prof. Benjamin B. Ferencz: We have reached a point where we will be discussing other measures of enforcing international law. Those who are expected to accept or comply with law must be aware that the laws are just. There can be no peace without justice and no justice without peace. What are the minimum standards necessary for human dignity?

As long as large numbers of people are deprived of water, food, health care, education and shelter, such deficiencies of the social order lead to international unrest - as they should. One of the obligations of those who seek a more peaceful world is to try to minimize injustices which exist in the world today. Lawyers, as always, have a vital role to play in creating the necessary legal structures to help eliminate human suffering and human strife.

Conference joined by:

Mr. Jack Yost
U.N. Representative of the World Association for World Federation.

We are fortunate in having with us a distinguished representative of the World Association for World Federation Mr. Jack Yost.

I'll ask him to tell us something about the vision of the world as seen by his organization so that we can consider it in the context of our search for a legal approach to a better world.

Jack Yost: We must have a vision for necessary improvements to take place in any international system. Changes depend upon public support which, in turn, requires some sort of a vision. For example, the problem of getting a world court with binding jurisdiction is very remote and abstract from the thinking of the American public and others because that issue doesn't exist in any context which they understand. Associations like the

111

WAWF must continue to hold up a vision of alternatives for a different kind of world.

People are motivated by myths and stories today as they were thousands of years ago. The tribal world was affected by such stories which gave meaning to life and explanations of things around them. When we watch our TV or movies we are being told stories and myths about our world and that influences how people feel about their lives. Since the United States media are influential throughout the world, the stories told in the American context are very important. Movies about the future almost always portray it as a disaster - nuclear holocaust, corporate big-brothers, individuals crushed by the state, etc. The evening news is full of war, terrorism, starvation and other evils. That story, fortunately, has lately begun to change.

The stories coming out of Eastern Europe and the striving of people there, in China and elsewhere, for human rights are a response to the kind of vision which World Federalists have always stood for. Human reality tends to become what people perceive it to be. What we believe is possible has an enormous affect on what actually happens. That's why stories and myths are so important.

My job as a non-governmental organization at the United Nations is to talk to diplomats about specific ways to strengthen international law. I try to communicate a feeling and a vision to "realists." What is "real" is what people believe is possible. They must be convinced that there are solutions, that there are alternatives, that the world in fact can be organized differently even if it's a huge problem. Human beings are inventors of systems. It is in this context that specific initiatives like the Decade of International Law has to be placed. It is a response to the yearning of human beings for a different kind of story - that progress is possible. Governments are beginning to respond to this new "myth" symbolized by the image of the planet as seen from space. We are becoming a planetary species. That is more than a new epic - it is an evolutionary breakthrough.

The energy that can come out of people all over the world working together to solve common problems is unparalleled in history. A faint echo can be seen in the Renaissance when new energies and new ideas were unleashed. The Decade of International Law is a call for us to get to work on building the specific architecture that we need for our common home on the planet. And governments are beginning to respond.

Prof. Benjamin B. Ferencz: A fresh and optimistic point of view is very welcome. It was good of you to remind us that new stories and new myths influence our society today. Believing that something is real encourages people to make it real, and human beings *can* solve human problems.

Dr. Galina Shinkaretskaya: I believe we have heard a very reasonable voice from Mr. Yost. He has a program of how to achieve the goal he seeks. I would like to know more about his vision for a future world.

Jack Yost: I don't really care exactly how the future world is organized, as long as it is an organization based on fundamental federalist principles. You begin with the notion that power resides in the citizen. Only that power is delegated to another level of government which must be so delegated because it can only be dealt with effectively on the higher level. We need a lot more freedom, power and autonomy at the local level and regional level. We may need a moderate increase of power at the global level to cope with problems that can only be solved globally. We need a vast reduction of power at the national level. When I say power, I mean money and other resources. People should be able to spend their tax dollar on solving their own problems at the local level as much as possible.

We need to invent an economic and political system at the global level that enhances the power of systems at the local level and at the same time is able to work efficiently at other levels to solve those problems that can only be solved at those other levels. Thus, we need some kind of global environmental protection agency. At the same time we need more resources at the local level so that people can begin solving local problems of recycling, renewable energy and things like that which can be dealt with very well locally.

Prof. Benjamin B. Ferencz: I think you are suggesting that we turn the pyramid upside down. At the moment, the government is the highest point and the people are the bottom. You suggest that we reverse the pyramid.

Jack Yost: That's right.

Dr. Galina Shinkaretskaya: It's astonishing how many people here are citing Mr. Yeltsin of the USSR in saying that the present power structure should be turned upside down. Mr. Yost sounds like he comes from the newly elected democratic Council at Moscow. They don't want to talk about socialism or capitalism but only about slow specific steps that move forward.

Prof. Benjamin B. Ferencz: I'm pleased to learn that the Moscow Council agrees with Mr. Yost's general concept of world federalism. Of course, the extent to which power actually resides in the citizen varies with the country. We should be moving toward a world where the citizen, whether represented by himself or an NGO or other agency, should be given greater power.

Prof. Rais A. Touzmohammad: I too am very satisfied with the statement by Mr. Yost. Our Association of Soviet Citizens Supporting Non-Aligned Human Concerns recently applied for membership in the World Federalist Association. The Non-aligned meeting in the Hague helped launch the United Nations Decade of International Law idea. Our Association is also preparing a program of action related to the Decade. We will be drafting documents for presentation to you and to the United Nations. We have a Declaration on Asian Pacific Legal Space worked out with the Asian Pacific Lawyers Association (APLA). It will include a declaration of peoples and minorities rights, of principles of international law for the Asian-Pacific region and a Convention on Principles for Resolving International Frictions in that region.

Prof. Benjamin B. Ferencz: Declarations are useful to alert public attention and perhaps support for a particular issue but they don't, by themselves, change the structure of the world. Lawyers will still be needed to outline the necessary specific legal instruments. Ideas for a federated world society go back hundreds of years. Henry IV, Immanuel Kant, Jeremy Bentham and a host of philosophers made such suggestions. You can go back to Christ, if you will, with the suggestion that "we are all our brother's keepers" as a form of world federalism. I'm sure that principle exists in other religions as well. So we need more than declarations if we are to advance to the declared goal.

Both Rais and Jack made reference to regional approaches. Can I ask whether we are trying to go too far this decade by talking about a *world* federation? Would it be easier to deal with *regional* federations first as part of an evolutionary process, Should we first be talking about a "European Home from the Urals to the Atlantic" and focus our structure on that more limited aspiration? Can we have planetary thinking now knowing that there are portions of this planet that are so under-developed that they can only be concerned with their immediate vital needs of food, water etc. Are we being too ambitious to even talk about world federalism today?

Dr. Galina Shinkaretskaya: Some time ago, the idea of world government became popular again in my country. But people began to realize that a world government structure would create the same bureaucracy which we now have in every state. It could revive a mechanism which is foreign to the rights of the individual. Nowadays, the idea of world government is not popular at all in my country. The Soviet people today are opposed to large governmental powers. The ideas of democracy have penetrated into our consciousness. Nations would only join a larger framework by their own free will. The idea of a world federation; however vague it might be, appeals to me more than one world state or one large state being divided.

Prof. Benjamin B. Ferencz: You seem to prefer the idea of a federation or loose confederation of more or less independent states because you fear a bigger bureaucracy if there were a dictatorship of the world. What about states seceding from a federation or union, such as the USSR. If that union were to break up into a number of independent states based on nationality or ethnicity because they were coerced into joining the USSR how could you get them to be part of a world federalist movement?

Jack Yost: Whenever one starts talking about reform at the global level you have the kind of fear among people reflected by your question. It is a big stumbling block. People are afraid of big government and they have every right to be afraid because the experience of it has been a very

115

negative or disastrous one. It's a terrible mistake, however, to take the nation state as the model for what a world state should be like.

The nation state is out of control. It's bloated, it's over-extended and it's trying to solve all kinds of problems which it has no business handling - such as the problem of world security. I call it the "fat man" government. Local and regional governments are being squashed by the enormous fat bureaucracy which sits above it. We must put the fat man on a crash diet and put a little more power on the global level and a lot more freedom, power and autonomy on the local level.

Whatever you call it, what we are really seeking is a system that works. We should not use words or descriptions that scare people. If they can be presented with a compelling alternative they will be more likely to change. Otherwise they will stick with the status quo no matter how bad it is.

Dr. Rose Cooper: I fully agree with that. I don't think people are ready to form any new kind of world organization. What they are ready for is to continue to have a vision: "If you don't have a dream how can it come true?" They want to understand what world peace would be like and how it can be accomplished. Then they may be able to act on it and put it into effect. You can not super-impose something that people are not ready to accept. That would be looking for more problems than solutions.

Sandra Bendfeldt: I agree with Jack about the importance of a new vision or "mythology" which is what people can be moved by. Do you have new descriptions or words that are more acceptable than "World Federalism?"

Prof. Benjamin B. Ferencz: Would you also answer whether regional organizations would be a more realistic way to visualize what is acceptable? How about a new name for it something like A Regional Association for the Promotion of Common Interests?

Jack Yost: Mr. Gorbachev spoke about a "common European home" which sounds quite appealing. A metaphor of a common home for the planet where all persons are fed and sheltered may be a powerful and

116

good idea. We will build this common home by building *regional* homes since functional agencies on the regional level are extremely important. In the near future, for example, we are not going to see a World Human Rights Court, but we may have more of them on a regional basis in different parts of the world. Later there may be a central court to reconcile different opinions that may arise among the regional courts.

The Coming European "Home"

Prof. Benjamin B. Ferencz: If we focus on the European scene today we see that there are several components of such a "home" already in place. The foundation has been laid by the Council of Europe. The European Community was originally an economic union. NATO, which developed later, was a military security alliance composed primarily of western European states. Confronting that was the Warsaw Treaty Organization, a military alliance for the Eastern states. In the Helsinki Accords, the Conference on Security and Cooperation in Europe (CSCE,) many European states reached agreement about principles designed to protect human rights and certain national boundaries. Those three different types of entities are already on the scene.

The European Community is pretty well integrated in terms of cultural background, economic standards and similar values. Can we, as lawyers, take these component parts and use the best of them for the purpose of structuring a new federation or confederation or association or whatever you may call it - a new society for Europe?

For example, the economic problems might be dealt with by an expanded European Economic Community. The security concerns could be handled by the military minds or structures of NATO or Warsaw Pact or some combination of the two. Environmental concerns might be dealt with by a new European Environmental Agency. Human rights concerns could be dealt with by the existing mechanisms such as the Helsinki principles and existing human rights courts and other agencies. The European Parliament might have a coordinating or supervisory function. These are things which lawyers can do by using the existing statutes and structures and modifying them as necessary to be adapted to the expanded area or region to be encompassed. Can we do it?

Prof. Rais A. Touzmohammad: May I note that you yourself noted that declarations alone are not sufficient. To gain acceptance for a European home we would have to propagate the ideas among the people and activate them. There are many non-governmental organizations but some of them are merely spokesmen for their governments which control and finance them. Recently, in the Soviet Union for example, dissident non-governmental organizations have begun to function. The Helsinki Watch Group is one of them, as is the one I am now associated with (SCSN). They can be very useful in propagating international law on the national level.

Dr. Rose Cooper: Education itself is the first step, the base. But we must follow it up with something practical. The public must hear things it can understand and visualize and then it must have some practical structure to show how it can be implemented.

Prof. Benjamin B. Ferencz: Let me summarize what we need "to make the dream come true." Surely we must educate the public, as you say, for their support is essential. But we must also be practical. We can begin with the important declarations that already exist, make them more specific, use the existing structures where they are usable, improve them where improvement is needed, discard those that serve no useful purpose and, as international lawyers, show specifically how we can move toward a more peaceful world where the house of the people will, one day, be in place.

Revisiting the International Court of Justice

Prof. Benjamin B. Ferencz: We have already had some discussion about improving the International Court of Justice, but in some of our off-the-record-discussions today some of the points made were so interesting that I have asked our colleagues to review it again. Dr.Galina Shinkaretskaya of the Institute of State and Law in Moscow is the author of an article on the subject, which was published in *Perestroika and International Law*, a book published in 1990 by the Edinburgh University Press. The title was *"Adherence to the Jurisdiction of the International Court of Justice."* I'm going to ask Galina to give us a brief resume of Soviet views, how they have changed and how they may change in the future.

Dr. Galina Shinkaretskaya: As early as the end of the last century, the Russian science of international law was highly developed. Russian scholars were at the cradle of the international court of justice. The first big book published on this in the world was by a Soviet scholar named Tamarowski. An Estonian, Martens, was responsible for the drafts which led to the Hague Conventions of 1899 and 1907. After the 1917 October revolution, the idea of international jurisdiction was propagated and the Lenin government suggested that special cases could be taken to international arbitration.

It was the western powers of the United States, UK and Japan which rejected arbitration regarding a few disputes with the Soviets which arose at that time. Ideological enmity led to a strict separation of the Soviet world and the capitalist world. I feel this split was one of the reasons which led to the second world war. The lack of a desire to cooperate in the matter of international juridical jurisdiction reflected the general reluctance to collaborate with the USSR.

Prof. Benjamin B. Ferencz: Sorry to interrupt, Galina, but I'm having a little difficulty with your heroic portrayal of the Soviet Union as the originator of the idea of arbitration. Cicero and Grotius and many others had also argued for arbitration. Can I get your view on the contemporary practice regarding the use of special chambers by the International Court of Justice which is a form of arbitration. Does it have real prospects and should chambers be restricted to interpretation of certain specific treaties only or should it be a general practice?

Dr. Galina Shinkaretskaya: Let me explain the position of our two countries before the advent of Perestroika which was a dividing line. The USSR formerly rejected the compulsory jurisdiction of any international bodies. Only about 15 treaties had provisions giving the International Court of Justice jurisdiction to interpret the treaty. Only about 20 treaties provided for international arbitration.

The United States seemed to accept jurisdiction of the International Court of Justice to interpret a much larger number of treaties and in fact went to the Court in a number of cases. The Connolly Reservation to Art. 36 (2) of the International Court of Justice statute, however, deprived the court of its compulsory jurisdiction in fact. Your own authority Thomas Franck has a similar opinion. Once the compulsory jurisdiction was in essence rejected by the United States there was no need for any change in United States relations to the Court.

Before Perestroika came to the USSR, I had been working for 10 years on problems of the International Court of Justice and no one would publish even an article on it. After Perestroika, our Foreign Ministry not only began to listen to the scholars, but began to steal their ideas. We became willing slaves working for peace for our country.

Suddenly, there was an article in Pravda by Gorbachev on 17 Sept. 1987 (which I read faithfully as a member of the communist party of the USSR, not to be confused with the new communist party of the Russian SSR, which is Stalinist and right-wing) and it dealt with realities and guarantees for a secure world. Gorbachev proposed that the USSR accept the compulsory jurisdiction of the International Court of Justice. It was incredible to me that a state would accept such jurisdiction unconditionally.

The International Court of Justice was patterned after the earlier Permanent Court of International Justice (PCIJ) which was based mostly on the UK system of law, rather than that of the United States or the USSR, and therefore it was understandable that not every state would accept it even though it could be a very good tool for settling disputes. When Mr. Scheverdnaze, our Foreign Minister, referred to the new Soviet view about the International Court of Justice at the General Assembly he referred to acceptance of compulsory jurisdiction along with other members of the

Security Council "on mutually satisfactory conditions." That was a sound approach. Reciprocity is one of the fundamental conditions for any judicial settlement or foreign relations agreements. It is more realistic and hence more likely to be fruitful.

At the General Assembly, Mr. Gorbachev said that the USSR was ready to accept the compulsory jurisdiction of the International Court of Justice regarding a number of human rights treaties but "on mutually acceptable conditions." The change was a logical consequence of Soviet turning toward the rule of law or *Rechtsstaat* by which they introduced international law as the leading factor in international relations. I think it was a decision on the highest political level to move away from the previous system.

I see that conclusion confirmed in the way the Foreign Ministry works today. The steps are not very big and not very quick but it is the introduction of law as the basis for international relations. Of course, those of us in the legal field were shocked by the change but it was a joyful shock. Without a future rule of law in international relations there is no future at all.

Prof. Benjamin B. Ferencz: Do you think the Soviet Union might also be persuaded to accept international criminal jurisdiction?

Dr. Galina Shinkaretskaya: Yes.

Prof. Benjamin B. Ferencz: That's very encouraging. Great Britain, France, the USSR and the United States were able to accept that at Nuremberg and once again the subject of such a court is being debated at the International Law Commission. We have seen in the past that the arrogance of power prevented states from turning to judicial settlement of major disputes. They preferred to rely on force - a very dangerous alternative in the nuclear age. We now see the beginnings of change. In what direction should we now be moving and what can we as lawyers do to accelerate that movement?

Dr. Galina Shinkaretskaya: I don't think the prospects are either excellent or bad. Despite the skepticism expressed by Paul Szasz when we discussed the agreement of the United States and USSR regarding International Court of Justice jurisdiction concerning certain treaties, there is a new trend. As we look at how the International Court of Justice is now being used, we see that the whole court is not being used as much as the new special chambers. Many states, retaining their sovereignty, are nevertheless increasingly providing that treaties will be interpreted by the International Court of Justice and they are honoring their obligations to accept the decisions reached. Thus we see that it has become part of the reality in the world that states are accepting the introduction of legal norms and law in international relations.

The first new Soviet initiative was that all Security Council members agree to accept the compulsory jurisdiction of the International Court of Justice on mutually acceptable conditions. But it was also indicated that even if the other members declined, the United States and USSR should enter into such an obligation on a bilateral basis. They are working on that and are also reviewing the procedural problems. They were trying to set a pattern which other Security Council members might then also accept. I am therefore quite optimistic about how it will develop. The two governments are getting ready to allow an independent body to judge their actions. This is a very important development in the acceptance of the rule of law.

Jack Yost: Let me play the devil's advocate. Do you see this recent negotiation to accept the special chambers of the court as something which may also be a step backwards, as the British have alleged?

Dr. Galina Shinkaretskaya: I don't know.

Prof. Benjamin B. Ferencz: The British have often said something was a step backward when they opposed it. They did the same with the definition of aggression, which they said would be dangerous because it would show the way to commit aggression. States which are conservative will be inclined to oppose change. When the PCIJ was first created, the British were most explicit in saying that they wanted the jurisdiction to be voluntary and not compulsory. They, like the Soviets, saw it as an intrusion on their sovereignty.

The important conclusion for us is that this great iceberg is beginning to melt a little bit on the surface. Beneath the surface, the ice is still there, but if we chip away at it long enough, as people, as non-governmental organizations as World Federalists, as Soviet scholars who see change as desirable in the interest of their own country and the world, then, perhaps one day in the not too distant future, we will accept the principle that rather than killing each other we will allow an independent body to decide disputes by peaceful means.

An Evolutionary View of World Needs

Prof. Benjamin B. Ferencz: In order to obtain maximum compliance with international law it must be clear that the rules to be enforced are fair to all. Human beings throughout the globe should all be entitled to minimum standards of human dignity if they are expected to abide by the rules. Do we
have a proper perspective of how that can be attained?

Conference joined by:

Robert Muller:
Former U.N. Assistant Secretary-General.

We are very fortunate to have with us a man who has had vast experience at the United Nations. For many years, he was an Assistant Secretary General, responsible for overseeing the work of many departments.
He is Robert Muller who has now retired from the United Nations although he remains as a valued adviser. He is also the unpaid Chancellor
of the University for Peace which is located in Costa Rica. He is the
author of very many books dealing with world peace. A recent one is *Most
of All They Taught Me Happiness.* Another one is *What War Taught Me
About Peace.* In 1982, Doubleday published his book *New Genesis:
Shaping a Global Spirituality.* All of his writings are very spiritual. They are
full of wisdom, humor, and ideas of all kinds drawing upon his vast experience. I have asked him to give us the benefit of his views and to tell us
what we as lawyers, as citizens, as non-governmental organizations can
do to make this a better world.

Robert Muller: My entire life has been dominated by a contradiction between my own approach to life and the society into which I was born. As a
child I thought that life was *Gottlich - divine. I was in love with nature and*

125

I was born near Malmedy in Belgium. It had been German before 1918 and my parents came from Alsace Lorraine which had also been German. My grandfather had five nationalities in his lifetime— without leaving his village. Living on the border, I saw the most incredible things which contradicted my own sense of life. From my window I could see the French Maginot line and watch the Germans build an Adolf Hitler village on the other side. The Germans wanted to put us into the army but I escaped and went into the French underground. My father was put in prison.

When I saw the nonsense of war between two civilized countries like France and Germany, I decided to work for peace. My father, who had been a hat maker and who wanted me to be a doctor, thought I was crazy. But I decided to study law and managed to get a position with the United Nations when I wrote an essay on world government. Although I held a doctorate in law, I came to the conclusion that law alone wouldn't make it. Law was an expression of existing values and the world would not change under the impact of law but would, I thought, change under the impact of economics. I became much more interested in economics than law.

My experience has confirmed my feeling about law. In my opinion, the International Law Commission is totally retrograde. I was involved in a few legal problems at the United Nations. For example, during a wave of hijackings of aircraft I had to prepare a speech for Secretary General U Thant. I suggested that he propose the establishment of a criminal court against hijacking. He made the speech and it created quite a scandal, but it caused the major powers to hasten to ratify the various treaties against hijacking which had been hanging in the air at the time. That's when I made the acquaintance of Ben Ferencz since I knew that he had similar views on the need for international criminal jurisdiction.

There were several other cases in which I also proposed the creation or use of international courts of justice. I believe that we need a World Court of Justice, like the European Court, where *individuals* can be protected against abuse by the state. It's an idea that was endorsed by a large gathering of young people in Strasbourg when they recently celebrated the 200th anniversary of the French Declaration of Human Rights. Young people are sick and tired of the sovereignty of states. They have a completely different view of humanity and of the planet.

An Evolutionary View of World Needs

If the Soviet Union and the United States do not wake up, they are going to be left completely behind. The Europeans have already decided to go ahead and create a world community. Read Jean Monnet's memoirs. At the end he says: "This is only the beginning." The nation state is no longer capable of dealing with the world's problems. The European Community will be the beginning of a world community.

I have written to President Bush, whom I knew from his days at the United Nations, and warned him that the United States may miss the opportunity to create a world community around the United Nations. Every Latin American country wants to become a member of the European Community. The Africans too are eager. I make a prediction that by the year 2000, the word "European" will have disappeared. Be it in outer-space or any other field there is an ingredient of a world community being born. There is a chance to use the United Nations as the center for a world community and if the United States does not seize that opportunity the Europeans will do it themselves.

For many years at the United Nations I was involved in the economic field. I have discovered that at the present moment that too is dead. We have come to a point in the evolution of this planet where everything is changing very fundamentally. Governments and people are facing events which are unprecedented. I have witnessed them all: the energy crisis, the population explosion, the environmental crisis and I see the new crises coming such as the world aging problem which will be a sociological catastrophe. The breakdown of the human immune system is another. Humans have existed for thousands of years with the notion that the planet existed to serve humans. Now a total revolution is taking place. Now it is no longer humanity that is priority number one but it is the earth itself.

At a time when developing countries have not yet reached a decent standard of living and justice - aggravated by the population explosion which is a problem by itself - the top priority has become the preservation of the planet to which all humans are subordinated. "Earth Days" go far beyond concern only with environment. A new awareness is moving in on us with tremendous speed. I think this is at the root of the recent changes in Soviet policy. They must have come to the conclusion that the world is changing so rapidly and drastically that being concerned about their position in Afghanistan is junk. While nations are worrying about the Middle East and other areas, the whole planet was going to pieces around them.

When the Secretary General asked all nations to review the status of the United Nations after 40 years of experience, the USSR did it very thoroughly. They soon shifted to a completely new foreign policy. We are now in a revolutionary state, like the time of Voltaire and Rousseau. They faced a political system where kings and aristocracy were hanging on when change was needed. The Encyclopedists assembled an inventory of knowledge, just as the United Nations is doing today, and artists and philosophers led a revolution against Napoleon and the power politicians of the time. We have exactly the same situation now. It's also a bit like the Renaissance when the middle ages were going to pieces and you had the Dante's and others who came up with a cosmic view.

We must go beyond the legal age and the economic age which have been left behind by more urgent events. As we approach the year 2000 we may be coming back to a kind of philosophical age. We must think about what we are doing to this planet and how we should manage it and relate to it and what our role is in the cosmos. Just look at what we are doing to the various species which inhabit this planet. Every five hours a species becomes extinct. When you think that it took millions of years to produce the miracle of a species and we, like idiots, just let them disappear.

We waste our time in stupid conflicts about nationalities, religious wars and things like that and place atomic bombs around the planet—*We should be ashamed!* The leaders of nations today are global dwarfs not to understand what the real issues are for the future of our planet. Things are moving very fast. There is growing recognition that there is a responsibility not merely towards the nation but also towards the earth. They have not yet understood that they also have a responsibility towards the cosmos.

We shall see fundamental changes. The field of law will have to consider the changes and accelerate them. I am very optimistic. This consciousness of our planetary destiny is growing rapidly. In the General Assembly, environment and climate are priority number one - more important than any political issue.

An Evolutionary View of World Needs

As we approach the next millennium we shall see, in 1992, the birth of the political community in Europe, the 20th anniversary of the first large environmental conference and the year of outer-space. In 1994, we shall have the "Year of the Family." In 1995, there will be the 50th anniversary of the United Nations. In 1996, there will be the Second World Congress of Religions where all religions of the world will seek to determine their commonality and the role of the human being in the cosmos and eternity. Then we have the year 2000. I am working to try to get the whole world prepared to consider what changes we need in order to move intelligently into the next millennium. The media are wild about it already.

I think we will be saved in the nick of time. Although the problems are increasing in severity, a time comes when there is a crisis and it continues to get worse for awhile and then there is a reversal. Governments react when they get scared - like children who react only after they have burned their fingers. In my 40 years at the United Nations, I have seldom seen anything done out of intelligence and foresight. When a crisis came it was followed by action. A satellite had to fall out of space before nations were ready to have a conference on how to deal with what was happening in outer-space. The environment crisis and the energy crisis are other examples.

I have two recommendations:

First, the political system of this planet is obsolete and disastrous. It has no justification whatsoever any more. It is being battered from the inside with requests for autonomy and it doesn't move intelligently towards the higher level. It has a double battle—inside and outside. One should think of the way in which human society should be organized to take care of this planet. We need a new political philosophy and a new political organization along planetary lines.

[In a preface I've written to the revised edition of *Planethood* by Ben Ferencz and Ken Keyes, I hypothesize about an invasion from outer-space. The invaders would say we must be kidding by the way we run things on earth.]

I think a strengthened United Nations will be necessary. Governments are wrong not to support it. If nations make the United Nations work well they might remain as administrative units of this planet. If the system doesn't work, nations will be in deep trouble. Those who now demand autonomy are saying that they can do as well as the present managers. In my book *What War Taught Me About Peace*, I have an essay about the year 2010. I argued that people should get together and begin to discuss the new political organization of our planet.

Second, you can force people to do things through law but you can also have them do things because they believe in them. The second great step we need is improved education. Young people must be educated along the right lines. Today it is nationalistic and ideological. This is obsolete. We must think of the human family as a whole.

Law is important to force people to comply with the ethic embodied in world law which still has to be developed. It is being developed by the United Nations in many areas. I have recommended that instead of international law we should have world law or global law. This is already mushrooming in the laws governing the seas, outer-space etc.

People will abide by law if they are correctly educated. I have been promoting a world core curriculum which has been adopted by many schools. In it the child learns that the nation state is no longer number one. The child must think of humanity as a whole. As citizens of the planet they will act responsibly in their personal and institutional lives.

This is my *crie du coeur*, my appeal to make you feel the urgency and need for change. When, many years ago at the United Nations, I proposed such changes people thought I was crazy. When the first World Conference on Environment was held it was called mockingly "The Bird Watcher's Conference." We must see things in an evolutionary perspective. It's something marvelous once we see our responsibilities in global terms.

Prof. Benjamin B. Ferencz: Thank you very much Dr. Muller for that very stimulating and challenging visionary view of the planet and cosmos. I'd welcome the observations of our Soviet friends.

Prof. Rais A. Touzmohammad: I am very much impressed by Dr. Muller's vision. I recall as a Muslim child in Uzbekistan that my grandparents told me that I was only one grain of sand and that my future was predicted by the stars. Now, apparently in the Soviet Union some of the officials are feeling the same way. One of our great academicians, Vladimir Vernadsky, advanced the idea of the "Noosphere" (that human reason could influence planetary development). That is now becoming reality.

What I may suggest as a lawyer is that we make humanity as a proper subject of the law of the future, not merely people or peoples or states or individuals but humanity as a whole. World law will deal with the universe and humanity as one component of it. The cosmos and outer-space can be proper objects of legal research. We have already started along that path and it will grow.

Sandra Bendfeldt: Let me mention the concept of the "common heritage of mankind" which seems to be out of style today. Can we still make it viable law? If it was originated by the Soviets, it was viewed with skepticism in the west and was therefore not as applicable to planethood or planetary interests as it should be.

Prof. Rais A. Touzmohammad: That concept reflected immense progress.

Robert Muller: The common heritage idea has gone very far and was accepted by the Democrats in the United States and may have been rejected by Republicans on political grounds. Very few people know that in 1982, the United Nations adopted a World Charter for Nature where the rights of nature are spelled out. There are some countries that are not eager to promote it because it might not be in their own interest.

131

Prof. Benjamin B. Ferencz: Robert Muller is a man dedicated to world peace. He has the "fire in the belly" which drives him in his striving for a wiser, more humane and more compassionate planetary and cosmic view of the problems we have been addressing. He is the Robert Schuman for our future and a new revolutionary who may lead us to a new renaissance of humanity. He has written an introduction for the new edition of the book Planethood which reflects similar ideas. He has been a great educator and his call for improved education and new thinking is most important.

Of course, you cannot move forward without changed legal structures as well. Law is only one small component in a much more complicated process but it's a component which we as international lawyers should not neglect. May I again convey our deep appreciation to Robert Muller for enlightening us with his wisdom.

Dr. Galina Shinkaretskaya: I was deeply impressed by your ideas which seem to be very vivid and profound. I was also happy to hear a high official of the United Nations with such fresh visions of the problems faced. I could feel the sincerity in his soul. This gives me new hopes for the future.

Prof. Benjamin B. Ferencz: On that happy and hopeful note I thank all of you for participating in this conference. Tomorrow, we shall meet at the United Nations for a review and critique of the conference thus far.

Conference Review Held at United Nations Headquarters

Conference joined by:

Lucy Webster:
U.N. Department of Disarmament Affairs.

Richard Hudson:
Center for War/Peace Studies.

B. G. Ramcheron:
United Nations

Prof. Benjamin B. Ferencz: As we meet here this morning at the United Nations, we have with us Ms. Lucy Webster of the United Nations Department of Disarmament Affairs. As Coordinator for the periodical "Disarmament" she is one of the most informed people dealing with that subject. We are also joined by Mr. B.G. Ramcheron from the Secretary General's Office for Research and the Collection of Information.

We have also been joined by Mr. Richard Hudson, the Executive Director of the Center for War/Peace Studies whose ideas for a "binding triad" to make the General Assembly more effective were considered during our earlier deliberations.

Outline of Prior Discussions

Since they were not present at the earlier meetings, may I outline briefly what we have been discussing. We began with the assumption that there were no ideological conflicts between the super-powers. As lawyers, we began to consider what changes had to take place in order to have the rule of law prevail in international affairs.

We considered three basic topics: 1 - The creation of binding norms of international behavior, 2 - The peaceful settlement of disputes and 3 - Enforcing international law. We reviewed the emergence of new laws, the evolution of international courts and the problems of managing the planet via the United Nations, and the difficulties of disarmament and arms control. We considered economic sanctions, United Nations peacekeeping forces and the problems of creating social justice in the world.

We were fortunate in being able to discuss these problems with persons of great knowledge and varied perspective. Paul Szasz, with many years of experience in the United Nations Office of the Legal Counsel, is quite realistic and helped to bring me down from my lofty heights and yet to make practical suggestions about how progress could be made. Robert Muller, who is an even bigger dreamer than I am, gave us the benefit of his perspective as a former Assistant Secretary-General. He thinks in cosmic terms and thinks the present decision makers are planning the menu for cocktails while the Titanic is sinking. The environmental problems had already been expounded for us by Prof. Nicholas Robinson of the Pace Law School who is an outstanding authority on environmental law.

With the help of all these very knowledgeable experts as well as persons like "Ping" Ferry, the man behind the EXPRO (Exploratory Project on the Conditions of Peace) which produced many thoughtful publications on the subject, we had a good scanning of the problems. We were assisted by Galina Shinkaretskaya, from the Institute of State and Law in Moscow. who is a great realist. Being trained in the Soviet Union, she was quite aware of the difficulties. She reminded us that we were dreamers but because she is very polite and sweet she added: "but it's a beautiful dream." I hope that along the line she was infected by that dream. Professor Rais Touzmohammad is also from the Institute of State and Law in Moscow and he has been busily engaged in trying to bring the non-governmental organizations of nonaligned countries together to enhance the human rights of peoples throughout the world. Soviet experts from the Ukraine are expected later today.

This morning we will begin with our own internal critique. We will ask the participants what they learned from the conference thus far and where do we go from here. The newcomers will then be asked to share their wisdom with us in the light of their own experiences and what they have heard. Please be frank in giving us your criticism and suggestions. Let me begin with Galina.

Internal Critique

Dr. Galina Shinkaretskaya: You made it sound like I was the only realist among dreamers and that I focused only on things in front of me and could not see beyond the horizon. I admit that I am a realist and that's just the reason why we must think about what is happening beyond the horizon. A realist sees what is going on in the immediate vicinity and thus realize how dangerous the situation is and how the problems now have acquired a global character. Unless you understand that, one cannot find the way out of the danger.

As a citizen of the Soviet Union but also a citizen of the world, I can see how planetary thinking is also of great importance to my country. The situation in the USSR is difficult and the better the situation in the world will be the better it will be within my country. I am a twofold realist because I want to work not only for the globe but for my country as well.

The conference itself is only a drop in the ocean compared to the world view. Still, the ocean is composed of drops of water and the more such conferences the fuller will the ocean be and the greater will be the understanding among peoples and the closer we will come to finding the correct paths to take. Although there were not so many people present at this conference, I learned a lot. I learned that there are people, even across the ocean, who share my ideas and who speak the words I would speak. If people in different parts of the world can get together and share their views, progress can be made.

I don't like to fly too high in the sky. I think we should stand on the soil of reality and begin from there. The immediate purpose of this conference, and others like it, should be to educate people to think globally. We can also produce documents to influence the heads of state and other decision makers. We should let them know what people are thinking.

Prof. Rais A. Touzmohammad: I think this meeting was very fruitful. In addition to what Galina said, despite logistic obstacles, we have *met* and that in itself is important. In our exchange of views, we found out that most of our ideas are similar. We joined together in a common war for a peaceful and cooperative future - a goal sought by people throughout the world.

I think the information we gathered through our discussion should be disseminated and published. I think there is need to publish a whole series of brochures, written in simple language, dealing with International Law for a Peaceful 21st Century. Our Association (SCSN) is ready to publish the whole series in English in the Soviet Union. That would be most fitting for the United Nations Decade of International Law. It might take up to three years but with the help of the United Nations perhaps it could be widely circulated among the member nations.

I also suggest that the next meeting on these themes should be held in the Soviet Union, possibly in Kiev, next year. In the name of SCSN Soviet Citizens Supporting Nonalignment's Human Concerns I would like to invite the Pace Peace Center as well as other American associations with which you are connected to Moscow, or some other place, say next June to deal with the new trends in the world and international law.

In order to educate the people locally, we should arrange a series of lectures on international law and the strengthening of international relations. We may try to arrange it in some of our remote republics which otherwise will not have such information. I can help arrange it. The lecture themes can be human rights and international law, disarmament and others. The team of Pace Peace Center specialists and Soviet experts visiting the outlying republics will help carry out the first rule laid down by the United Nations Decade - to propagate international law.

Prof. Benjamin B. Ferencz: I was very pleased to hear that you are ready to publish such discussion in English in the Soviet Union. We will provide you with the tapes so that you can arrange that. It will be clear that we all share a common concern and a common interest in preserving the planet and ourselves. But it will require some changes before it can become a reality. Let me ask Paul Szasz for his criticism and suggestions.

Paul Szasz: I see peace in institutional terms. The United Nations is basically an adequate instrument to start the process. Now that the cold war seems to be ending, the Security Council should come into its own. We cannot eliminate the veto power but you may be able to arrange some redistribution of memberships, but if the world community is to be mobilized it will still have to act by general consent.

As for the International Court of Justice, it too does not need any major reform but it could use expanded jurisdiction which could be made compulsory in particular instances.

The organ that is most flawed is the General Assembly. The idea of one-vote-one-nation is considered democratic but is nothing of the sort. Democracy lies in the people and not in sovereign nations. An organization in which tiny states have the same vote as those with enormous populations can not make any meaningful decisions. Something has to be done either about the composition or the voting arrangements in the Assembly if the principal organ of the United Nations is to be taken seriously. How to do it is not easy since all weighting factors have their disadvantages. A combination, as proposed by Richard Hudson, might offer a solution.

As far as the Secretariat is concerned, I do not see a need for great reform. It might be better if the Secretary General's election were not subject to great-power veto.

We talked about other institutions that might be created, particularly a disarmament verification agency. That would seem to be called for. There is no doubt that if things continue as they do now there will be considerable cause for disarmament of all weapons of mass destruction, together with bilateral and international verification. It might be possible to combine several verification functions within a single agency and the International Atomic Energy Agency might be a useful model.

Other new agencies that one can foresee might be an International Environmental Agency and possibly a further enhanced Human Rights Agency and a Commissioner of Human Rights.

These are ways in which I think we can progress towards peace institutionally, slowly, and in an evolutionary rather than a revolutionary manner.

As for my critique of this conference, I must say that I'm not a great fan of conferences. The best work is done in private research. Conferences enable one to meet people and the format doesn't matter much. Editing these tapes won't be easy and the participants may have to be given the opportunity to edit their own portions.

Sandra Bendfeldt: Although I'm not a legal scholar, I do not believe that isolated research is adequate to bring about changes in the world. It leads to a breakdown of communication between people. Publications alone can not bring people together and change minds. We are stuck with old myths adhered to by nations and ethnic groups in a divisive way.

What I learned from this conference is that everyone in the room, in one way or another, foresees the breakdown of sovereignty and the arrival of a new conceptual organization of the planet. Beginning with the Europeans and the concept of a home from the Atlantic to the Urals a model is being prepared for the rest of the world. It is foreseeable that what we have now will be vastly changed and regional organizations, and perhaps even the understanding of *Planethood,* will be realized.

This conference, combined with my attendance at Roger Fisher's course on negotiating techniques has had a deep impact on me. He speaks of a process of behavior modification and dispute resolution. It gives structure to common sense and has a productive result. These processes are useful to advance world thinking toward common and shared goals.

Prof. Benjamin B. Ferencz: Bringing people together is part of that process of understanding that we have common needs and share the same goals. In the last analysis we are all tiny specks on a great planet floating through space. Until we realize that we must all swim together or we will sink together we will not be able to create the institutional changes that Paul Szasz called for. It is a primary function of lawyers but they

138

alone can do nothing. The people have to be educated through a democratic process in democratic institutions.

My own reaction to the conference thus far is that it is only a beginning. I'm very satisfied with the conference. Being able to discuss very fundamental problems with legal experts from the Soviet Union is important. Even if the discussions could not be in great depth, it was sufficient to become aware of the problems and to suggest possible areas of improvement. We don't have to fix what is not broken. But where there is obvious need and we see that the system just doesn't work, change is needed.

We can see that in many areas the system *doesn't* work. We see starvation among millions of people in the world, we see environmental pollution, we see universal fear caused by the nuclear threat, we see constant wars taking place—all of which tells us that the present system doesn't work. It is time that those who are responsible for making it work recognize the reality and do something about it. That's what this conference is all about.

Need for a Comprehensive System

Prof. Benjamin B. Ferencz: We have again been joined by Jack Yost who is the United Nations Representative of the United States Association for World Federation. He was with us during our discussions in Pleasantville. Jack, give us your views about the utility of this type of conference where lawyers from the Soviet Union and the United States begin "brainstorming" about specific problems of world order.

Jack Yost: I agree that such discussions are important. We must continue to talk about specific methods for improving the international legal system and we need as much creative thinking as possible. Specific questions, like how to improve the world court and peacekeeping activities of the United Nations, and so on are necessary. But I think that a different kind of gathering is also needed in the future.

Everything is connected to everything else. This is often described as interdependence - a fuzzy word. It implies that we live on a planet where all systems are connected to all other systems. That means that tens of thousands of social and political systems which we have created are now

139

connected in an incredibly complex web. This has a tremendous bearing on how you solve problems. If the solution does not take into account the impact on other related systems, you may end up with more new problems than you've solved.

Because the problems are connected and because our ecology is deteriorating so rapidly, we must find solutions at the core of these systems quickly or we'll just be putting our fingers in the dike and not accomplishing very much.

We need discussions about strategic thinking, planning and implementation. We need to analyze what is happening throughout the network. If, for example, you have a conference only about law, I'm not sure how fruitful it will be unless it's in the context of the larger system. Recently, I went to a conference on development. High officials spoke mostly about past failures and a few lessons learned, but they did not deal with the complexities of the issue of development. There was a lack of fresh thinking.

I really don't know how you flip the world system into a new one that is benefitting everyone on the planet. Perhaps you could begin with a sample project such as taking one or a few small nations and set up a commission to study the problem in its many ramifications and come up with a comprehensive analysis of what it would take to make a change in say a ten-year period. It would require an analysis of the needs, the current resources, other resources that could be brought to bear, education, health, human rights, trade, corporate investment, internal democratic processes, corruption, agriculture, cultural differences, and all the other factors that might enter into a comprehensive plan to turn the system around.

To be realistic, what is required is creative thinking and material resources. We now lack such strategic plans or a workable model on which to base larger plans. Now, nobody, not even the United Nations, is thinking about managing the planet in such a comprehensive way.

Prof. Benjamin B. Ferencz: You have put your finger on one of the fundamental difficulties. Mr. Gorbachev put forward a Comprehensive Security Plan in his 1987 speech and further efforts at the United Nations, but it received scant consideration.

You are describing an enormous panorama; like a jigsaw puzzle, all of the pieces must be in place before the picture becomes visible. You see that also in the peace movement. It is scattered and the weakest component is perhaps the legal component. There is a strong religious component and educational component which are of course vital. But all of the pieces of the motor must be in place and running if the vehicle is to go forward. We are dealing with prototypes most of which, like the Wright brothers when they built the first airplane, are landing on their head. It takes going back to the drawing board and workshop.

You recently organized a conference, attended by Lucy Webster, Mr. Ramcheron, Prof. Louis Sohn and others, where we dealt with similar questions. Can you share with us some of the things you learned there?

Jack Yost: I think it was useful mainly as an opening shot. It was more or less a free-flowing brainstorming. As I indicated, it would be helpful if there could be a more analytical follow-up to consider, for example, all of the elements that currently exist in the area of security and peacekeeping to see how they and other existing agencies might more effectively be integrated into an improved system.

Prof. Benjamin B. Ferencz: That's exactly what we have been trying to do; to build on what we've got and try to make them better. I'd like to ask our Soviet friends to give us their views on what happened to Gorbachev's Comprehensive Security Plan that included so many vital components of what is required. The United States had opposed it in the United Nations.

Prof. Rais A. Touzmohammad: There was a group established in the Institute of State and Law to consider what might come out of it from an international point of view. We published a book on it which appeared the same month that Gorbachev announced the idea from the rostrum of the General Assembly. Then everything died down. In my opinion what happened was this: after we put forward a very comprehensive plan of four major changes based on Perestroika, Gorbachev then added the environment as a fifth point, the United States was not in favor of it. Without United States support it couldn't go forward so we dropped it and are no longer going forward with comprehensive plans. There were a few resolutions passed which, in essence, simply repeated United Nations Charter principles. I don't think we are again going to come out with a comprehensive plan. We will try to deal with it piecemeal. It seems to be easier to reach agreement that way.

Jack Yost: What you are saying is correct. If a major party like the United States is not willing to go along with a comprehensive approach to these very complex problems, then we are stuck and can't move forward. The Soviet initiative is useful because it puts forward a model, but how can you build a house if one of the builders doesn't want to participate? That's why I think we might do better to begin with a country in Africa or something like that as a smaller model. If it can be shown to work, then skeptics like the United States might get excited about it and be willing to apply it to a larger area.

Prof. Benjamin B. Ferencz: The United States, in fact, opposed any consideration of the 1987 Gorbachev plan. General Walters, our Permanent Representative at the time, reported to the Congress that "we have succeeded in defanging this pernicious Soviet attempt to subvert the United Nations Charter." When, the next year, the Soviet's came forward with a somewhat modified plan for tentative consideration, it was condemned by the United States as a "Trojan horse." I can see why the Soviets were discouraged and ready to give it up.

I would suggest that if one of the partners does not want to build the house then you proceed to build the house without the partner. The house *is* being built. It is called The European Home. Rather than going out to Africa, as Jack suggests, and building a new model in an area where the levels of development and culture are so different that it is not likely to serve as an applicable model, why not use the European Community as the appropriate model? That's already being built and all it needs are a few more bricks. Instead of walking away because one partner says: "I don't believe you and I don't trust you," we should go ahead and do the best we can without waiting.

Lucy Webster: The idea of a common European home is very important, particularly in the context of disarmament issues. If we can make the CSCE more effective it might be able to supplant the NATO presence by a presence from the Atlantic to the Urals or San Francisco to Vladivostok.

Thus an institution which includes the European states plus the United States and Canada may be extremely important.

There's another way to do an end run around the outdated thinking of certain leadership groups. We can go to the people.The United Nations norms of international law can play an enormous role if the people are educated to understand them better. The global norms, the status of their implementation and the different instrumentalities that already exist should be much better communicated to a broader public.

We should no longer be thinking about states with black boxes but rather as entities which are dynamic, where there are arguments within them and which are responsive to public demand. That's vital for implementation which is a process of what officials do and what the public urges them to do. The sociological basis for the political process has to be appreciated. The wide public must know that in the 1987 Gorbachev speech he was articulating the new basis for Soviet policy. It was the end of the bipolar system that existed before then, and the elimination of the traditional "enemy."

Prof. Benjamin B. Ferencz: In earlier sessions we discussed the need for making institutions, including the United Nations, more responsive to the voice of the people and the need for educating them and non-governmental organizations to assert their power. So we are grateful for your again reminding us of the importance of the people and the educational process as we move toward global thinking.

Richard Hudson: We can do both - look to a nation like Namibia as a model, which is off to a good start, and also think in comprehensive terms. It is difficult to predict the pace of change. In 1953, when the effort was started to establish the European Political Community, it consisted of six nations and was supposed to be superimposed on the European Defense Community. It fell apart when De Gaulle refused to go along. It will probably be around 1993 when the political operation of 12 European states will be formed - forty years later. A few years ago, I proposed that a World Space Organization be established on the site of the Berlin wall. Everybody thought I was out of my mind. Yet a few years later the wall came down.

143

I compare the United Nations to an automobile with square wheels. It's very difficult to move. But if it's the only auto you've got, you've got to try to do it. At the same time you should try to improve it. We at the Center for War/Peace Studies are working hard for a United Nations Verification Agency, which will not require an amendment to the Charter. It should be able to verify more than arms control agreements but also environmental and regional conflicts and so on. If it's limited to disarmament, it's chances are better.

We are also trying very hard to get the Binding Triad system introduced into the United Nations. We have a deadline of the year 2000 and we think we're making progress. We think it would solve the problems arising from the veto in the Security Council and the very un-representative voting system that now exists in the General Assembly.

One man's realist is another man's Don Quixote. I don't know whether I'm a Don Quixote or a hard-nosed pragmatist. I think I'm the latter and that's why I'm advocating the Binding Triad. Sometimes we need more than just band-aids but also major surgery. We are trying both.

Prof. Benjamin B. Ferencz: I'd like to greet some of our newly arrived guests. We have **Britt Kjolstad**, who is the Law Librarian at the United Nations. Without being able to build on the knowledge of the scholars who went before, we couldn't get anywhere. She has been most cooperative and helpful to all of us, including our present guests from the Soviet Union. I'd like to make it a matter of record that we are grateful for her help.

Gerald Mische has also just walked in. He and his wife Patricia are the founders of Global Education Associates - which in partnership with many other related peace groups has been doing great work in the field. They are the authors of a book called *Toward a Human World Order* which expresses the desire of all of us for a more humane planet.

Disarmament as Seen From the United Nations

Let us go now to the disarmament field. It is a most crucial one because the house is in danger of exploding. If we are unable to bring arms under international control we face the peril of dying not from environmental pollution but from a big bang which will end everything right then and there.

In our earlier discussions, we considered the possibility of setting up an arms census - a proposal made by the French after the first world war. It would tell us who has what and serve as the basis for controls as originally prescribed In the Covenant of the League of Nations. That would have to be coupled with an international agency to control armaments under a system which can be effectively verified.

Lucy Webster through her publications on disarmament keeps all of us informed of progress in the various disarmament efforts. Lucy, how does it look to you, what are the prospects, what needs to be done, what can *we* do?

Lucy Webster: The disarmament picture is somewhat mixed. The Conference on Disarmament (CD), which is going on in Geneva, is one of the important examples of the 40-member multilateral process. The prospects for arriving at a treaty banning the retention and production, as well as the use, of chemical weapons is close to completion.

There has also been a lot of bilateral work on disarmament between the United States and the USSR. It's also going along quite well. The START (Strategic Arms Reduction Talks) negotiations to reduce intercontinental strategic weapons have also been moving along but it doesn't seem likely that they will reach the original goals of 50% cuts. It may be between 10% and 30%. The Non-Proliferation Treaty, which will soon come up for review, comes to an end in 1995. Those states that have signed it have pointed to their contribution toward limiting nuclear arms but something more will have to be done to curb such weapons if they are to be kept in line. The INF Treaty was a step in the right direction.

The Partial Test ban Treaty is also up for review and possible amendment to convert it into a Comprehensive Test Ban Treaty. That would be of great importance since it would prevent modernization of nuclear weapons. If you can't test, it will accelerate the phasing out of the entire nuclear system of security.

Other concepts of "Defensive Defense" or "Strategic Defense" may be interim steps on the road toward a United Nations security system of comprehensive disarmament as originally envisioned, but seldom mentioned now.

Prof. Benjamin B. Ferencz: The most optimistic part of your report relates to the expected treaty to ban chemical weapons - something we have been expecting for years! The use of such weapons was banned in 1925 so that doesn't seem like much progress. You earlier said that if leaders won't do what they should, we should go directly to the people. Not being a diplomat, may I ask a very direct question: Is the United States a major stumbling block and how do you make an end-run around that?

Lucy Webster: I think that a comprehensive system of international security is a *sine qua non* of comprehensive disarmament. If everyone would insist upon making the United Nations and its peacekeeping capacities adequate you wouldn't have the excuse that weapons are needed for national security. That would require a total change in the present system.

Prof. Benjamin B. Ferencz: That's absolutely correct. No one will disarm as long as there is no effective system in place to settle disputes by peaceful means. We had the McCloy/Zorin agreed statement of principles calling for total disarmament under effective international controls. That had been accepted by the United Nations unanimously and although as Paul Szasz has just whispered, neither the United States nor the USSR really wanted it, it proposed a sensible legal system. Can we go back to that as a means of moving the disarmament process forward?

Lucy Webster: Certainly we have to get back to that. But it would require an attitude change among certain major military nations. Gorbachev has espoused precisely the principles we're talking about here so we can no longer blame the Russians. The United States espouses the principles too, but when it comes to the nitty-gritty of giving the United Nations power to handle it, the United States has serious reservations. These doubts are quite deeply based in leadership groups which I do not think reflect the views of the majority of the population but the general public is not sufficiently vocal or organized to counter the decision makers.

Prof. Benjamin B. Ferencz: What can we lawyers really do to make more effective the disarmament efforts that have been going on at the United Nations and elsewhere for many years and don't seem to be getting anywhere?

Lucy Webster: Lawyers can be a very important leadership group, particularly in the United States. The broad public must be made to realize that there really isn't any need for the vast military establishments and arsenals that we have. The people who hold the view that large military capacities are irrelevant have isolated themselves from credibility as far as the majority is concerned. Lawyers can be helpful in demonstrating that the peace movement is not just a small group of do-gooders who have rather irrelevant ideas.

The people who are respected in the various communities have to get involved and understand the issues. For example, at the moment it is important for leadership groups in the United States and the UK to understand that a vast number of people want to have a comprehensive test ban. These two nuclear weapons states have broken off the talks with the USSR regarding that. The governments are not clear what the public will is, although they do know that they must maintain nuclear capacity and that they must keep testing to maintain the nuclear deterrent system.

We must also challenge the concept of deterrence. Lawyers could be very important in doing that. Deterrence is widely perceived as a system which has worked to avoid major wars during the past 45 years at least between the superpowers. You could still have deterrence and sufficient defense with 90% reduction of nuclear weapons. What is needed is a real reduction to the level needed only to maintain internal security within states.

If you want comprehensive security you must get rid of the concept of deterrence. Lawyers who understand the role of international law in a security system which includes environmental, political and economic security

We must also challenge the concept of deterrence. Lawyers could be very important in doing that. Deterrence is widely perceived as a system which has worked to avoid major wars during the past 45 years at least between the superpowers. You could still have deterrence and sufficient defense with 90% reduction of nuclear weapons. What is needed is a real reduction to the level needed only to maintain internal security within states.

If you want comprehensive security you must get rid of the concept of deterrence. Lawyers who understand the role of international law in a security system which includes environmental, political and economic security must address the issue and say that we don't need a system which depends upon the threat of mutual assured destruction. We do not need deterrence and we do not need these weapons in any quantity such as we have today. Nuclear weapons can be totally phased out. They are no longer needed to offset the Soviet geopolitical advantage they had with conventional weapons that could be used on the land mass of Europe. That has changed and the threat that may have justified a counter-threat option no longer exists.

Lawyers should be able to argue logically that the whole basis on which the military confrontation that was built up over the years no longer exists and therefore the whole system needs to change. The corollary is that we must strengthen the peace systems of the United Nations.

Prof. Benjamin B. Ferencz: I appreciate your assumption that lawyers can persuade by logical arguments. The strongest argument *against* nuclear disarmament has been that the existence of nuclear weapons has maintained the peace. The logic of that is that if A (peace) exists while B (nuclear weapons) exists that proves that A is caused by B. Any first year student in logic will tell you that such reasoning is not logical. Since such distorted reasoning still prevails, I'm not so sure that logic alone will work.

Let me ask Rais a question. Lucy has noted that the armaments industry can exist because there is a presumed enemy and that the Soviet Union is disappearing as that enemy. The USSR under Gorbachev is beginning to disarm. Does the Soviet public have the same perception as here that money saved on arms can be used as a peace dividend to enhance so-

148

concept and that is quite new among international lawyers; that is the idea of confidence building. This is just the opposite of an arms race for reasons of deterrence. This is the system we must build in the future. People to people meetings, like ours, serves that purpose. I call you "Ben", you call me "Rais", you have invited me to your home and I have invited you to Kasakstan. That's confidence building. Gorbachev's visit to the United States and his personality serves to build confidence. That's much better than military deterrence.

Prof. Benjamin B. Ferencz: In addition to confidence building we need institution building and that's where lawyers are needed. We must create viable alternatives to the use of force and institutions which eliminate the inequities and injustices which provoke wars and other conflicts. Lawyers alone are not enough. Without the people you can do nothing. With the people, as you have seen in the USSR, almost anything can happen.

We also need institutions to make sure that desired changes take place in an orderly way. We must avoid the dangers and the chaos that comes with radical change if we do not have in place the structures for the peaceful reorganization of society. Robert Muller, who has just rejoined us, gave us a cosmic view of the changes needed. He has brought us not down to earth but up to the skies. "A man's reach must exceed his grasp, or what's a heaven for?"

We must look to theologians, to teachers and to men of vision to inspire the people. That's what the Mische's and other peace messengers are doing. Lawyers alone can't do it. They are terrible teachers. They are dull, usually only interested in getting a big fee and not much concerned with peace issues which don't pay. To be a Prophet of peace is very unprofitable. The mass media must be enlisted in our effort to educate and win the confidence of the people that a more secure and better world is possible without this devastating nuclear arms race. It will take some time but it is very urgent.

Robert Muller: Whenever I come to the United Nations I meet many old friends. Today, several of them asked me whether I was glad that what I had preached for so many years, and for which many regarded me as a little crazy, has now become reality. The only conclusion I can draw from that is that we must always be ahead of our time. We must always be beyond the current beliefs. We must always have dreams and visions and proposals. We must bring about change by making an indent in the lazy minds of those who live on the existing structures.

The other day some one read me a chapter in a book where I am labelled as a "specialist in impossibilities." I like that. I don't like to be involved in possible things. Once something becomes possible, I move out completely.

My wife Margareta once asked me why I didn't attend-with-my-wife any of the many United Nations world conferences in various parts of the globe. I said that I would never attend a conference that I had triggered. Some one must stay behind to think of the next world conference which may take ten or fifty years. We must always be ahead of our time. It was said that the United Nations Secretary-General must always be ahead of governments but not too much because he is a political man. All of you have no such restraints.

We must prepare for our worldwide entry into the next millennium in an intelligent way. The Pope is being asked to come to the United Nations in 1994 during the International Year of the Family to address the Family of Nations. Ideas have to be incorporated into new structures that will continue and give life to the ideas. The United Nations is a body of structures that go on and is ideally suited as a center for such structures. I have spent forty years trying to build one institution after another at the United Nations. The most magnificent institutions are those which have charisma and the United Nations is in the forefront. It embodies the ideals and dreams of all the peoples around this world.

In my book, the United Nations is the greatest institution ever established, and I am not alone in that view. A reporter once asked U Thant what was the most important event of the century and he immediately replied: "The creation of the United Nations." It is one of the great events of human history. As you go back to your countries remember that this is holy ground. This is the place where every great thinker of human history is becoming a reality. We have a responsibility not to let the people down and not to leave any stone unturned in order to get this planet into good shape and to make it a jewel in the universe as it is supposed to be.

Prof. Benjamin B. Ferencz: With those inspiring words about the United Nations, we close this meeting at the United Nations.

MEETING RESUMED AT PLEASANTVILLE WITH UKRAINIAN DELEGATION

Conference joined by:

Yuri S. Shemshouchenko:
Director of the Institute of State and Law, Kiev.

Vladimir V. Furkalo:
Deputy Chief of the Institute of State and Law, Kiev.

Vladimir I. Evintov:
International Law Department of the Institute of State and Law, Kiev.

Prof. Benjamin B. Ferencz: We are very fortunate this morning to have with us three representatives from the Institute of State and Law in Kiev, who have just arrived from the Soviet Union:

Yuri S. Shemshouchenko is the Director of the Institute, which is part of the Ukrainian Academy of Sciences. He is the author of many books and articles on international law and a leading authority on legal protection of the environment.

The Deputy Chief of the Institute, Vladimir V. Furkalo is also with us. He is an authority on arms control measures.

The third guest from the Ukraine is Vladimir I. Evintov, who is the Senior Research Fellow of their International Law Department and the author of many books and articles.

A Brief Overview

I am pleased that the representatives of the Institute of State and Law in Moscow, Prof. Touzmohammad and Dr. Shinkaretskaya, have already briefed you on our previous discussions. Let me again summarize. We dealt with strengthening the law of peace. That involved trying to find new concepts and consider new statutes that would help to create a peaceful world order. We have assumed that decision makers had put aside their past ideological differences and had asked us to help them build the new legal structures for peace. We talked about a new type of law - a law for the planet - a type of law that would serve the interests of every country since by serving the interests of the whole the parts would also be enriched.

We considered the existing international courts and other means for the peaceful settlement of disputes. Without a legal mechanism to settle disputes without the use of force the temptation, and indeed the necessity, to use force will remain. Our approach has been to use what already exists and seek improvements only where they are necessary.

The third major topic we addressed was how to improve the enforcement of international law. To begin with, we considered a system of management. In effect that meant looking at the United Nations for that is the only system of world management that we have. We talked about possible improvements of the General Assembly to make it more democratic and ways to make the Security Council more effective. We felt it might be time to review the fifty-year old prototype under which the world now operates.

We recognized that an essential component of international law enforcement is to bring armaments under international control. Yet, because everything is linked, no one will disarm until there is another system in place to settle disputes without arms. We spoke of an International Verification Agency, of more "transparency" and of a completely different approach to security, such as "defensive defense." We also asked how we could get to comprehensive and universal disarmament, as had been described in the McCloy/Zorin Accords of 1961, which had a great deal of support at the time.

We talked about alternative methods of enforcement by economic and other sanctions such as United Nations peace-keeping forces. Finally, we recognized that in order to obtain maximum compliance with a new system of international relations it would be necessary to be fair to all. That meant that some of the glaring inequities and injustices in the world today would have to be addressed and remedied. The abuse of the environment by some nations at the expense of others is one such problem which we considered in depth. Both Prof. Nicholas Robinson and Robert Muller of the United Nations gave us clear warning of the grave perils which we now face and which must be corrected if the planet is to survive.

I am going to ask Prof. Touzmohammad to comment on my summary and correct or add to anything that I have said in order to be sure that we have an accurate and fair presentation as a basis for our continuing discussions.

Prof. Rais A. Touzmohammad: Your briefing was fair and comprehensive, as usual. I would like to add two points which were omitted. The first relates to the increasing role of non-governmental organizations in the process of law making and law enforcement. The second relates to the increasing role of moral precepts in the law making process as the basis of international norms in the future. I would also like to draw attention to the role of humanity as the subject of international law. This may be a new norm in the existing system of norms and principles which start with domestic laws and then move on to laws of humanity as such.

Prof. Benjamin B. Ferencz: Rais, I very much appreciate your adding these points. You are quite correct in drawing attention to the change in our moral perceptions on behalf of humanity. We must move away from the present system of stabbing and grabbing to one of caring and sharing. These perceptions have inspired many non-governmental organizations to take a more active role in the process of creating a more stable world.

Galina, I would appreciate it if you would, with the same candor that you have always shown at these meetings, add or subtract or correct anything that has been said.

Dr. Galina Shinkaretskaya: Now I can understand how useful these meetings have been for me. I seem to be getting more and more clever. I have just been struck with the idea that if we are going to have one humanity living in one society then there would be no international law at all, or state law or constitutional law. What would there be to rule the behavior of individuals who would be living in the spirit of humankind and planethood? It might be something like what we now call general principles of law or general principles of morality. I agree with my colleague, Prof. Touzmohammad that morality seems to be coming to the forefront of the tasks we have before us. Being a realist, I should say that we have been discussing international law in a transitional period.

What sanctions should be taken against those unwilling to accept this new order? If there are groups who are unwilling to join the spirit of Planethood and humankind perhaps we should not use force against them. I shall consider this in my future work.

I would also like to work on the idea of an international court with compulsory jurisdiction to deal with environmental problems and which would require states to submit reports on their behavior and its impact on the environment.

Prof. Benjamin B. Ferencz: You are right to suggest that what we are working on is international law in a transition period; to bring about the transition that we seek. Rais, elsewhere referred to law being like the banks of a stream and it's the function of the lawyer to build the banks and guide the stream toward a better society.

You are right to raise the question of how to coerce those who won't accept the change and there will always be such people. You would have to use the force that is necessary just as the policeman takes the criminal to jail against his will. There are other non-forceful means as Mahatma Ghandi has demonstrated. Some communities have used passive resistance to defeat an aggressor. Economic sanctions, the economic weapon envisaged by the Covenant of the League of Nations didn't work. It had to be improved.

The idea of an enforcement agency for environmental problems is a very acute one. Perhaps it's as important as having nuclear disarmament. Perhaps the Security Council should deal with that or another Council specializing in that problem and having enforcement powers.

Let me engage our friends from the Ukraine on the original topic of strengthening the law of peace. What law is necessary for the transitional movement from the present chaotic state of international affairs (as described by Secretary General Perez de Cuellar) to the more peaceful world that we seek?

Prof. Yuri S. Shemshouchenko: [Translated] The questions being discussed here are of vital importance for mankind. This conference represents a fine beginning for the future when we can continue to discuss all our common problems together.

The Right to a Healthy Environment

Prof. Yuri S. Shemshouchenko:I would like to comment on the right of all human beings to a healthy environment. Unfortunately, I couldn't be here when my friend Prof. Robinson addressed this subject during the early days of this conference but we have considered the difficulties in the past. I would like to consider the role of international and domestic law in solving this problem. I would also like to consider how this right can be brought to life, enforced and guaranteed.

In 1972, the Stockholm Declaration on the Environment was adopted. It was declared that every human being has the right to a healthy environment. But the Declaration had no binding-force it was not obligatory. Perhaps as a result of that, there were no changes made in the domestic legislation of the participating countries. This right is not reflected in the constitution of the United States, the USSR or any other state   even though I consider it one of the fundamental rights of human beings. Nor does it appear in the Declaration of Human Rights or other international instruments. That's why I believe that this right should be codified at the international level.

How do we go about it? In 1992, there will be a United Nations Conference on Environment and Development. We should use that occasion to adopt a Declaration or work out an international agreement dealing with environmental protection and development. In that instrument the rights of human beings to environmental protection should be codified. It might inspire other states to follow that example by introducing the same principle into domestic legislation.

Prof. Benjamin B. Ferencz: That's a very constructive suggestion. Your proposal that we try to do something in connection with the pending 1992 Conference has stimulated the thought that perhaps we should also try to link our environmental concerns with the pending Draft Code of Crimes against the Peace and Security of Mankind, which is now before the International Law Commission. Perhaps environmental pollution should be listed as a specific offense which would be punishable so that individuals and states which violate these international norms would be held to account.

Creating a New International Legal Order

Dr. Vladimir I. Evintov: First let me thank you for considering and discussing my book during your earlier meetings. The book is dedicated to the international community and legal order. I am sure that humanity is not yet the subject of international law. To be realistic, we must recognize that the international community is not yet a community of nations but a community of states. Peoples can not yet participate in the deliberation of international law. We must create conditions to make that possible.

One of the ways to create such conditions is via public opinion. I think that it is very necessary to create a commission of lawyers for this work of international management. They should negotiate with states to inhibit actions which contradict international law. We see, for example, the work of the International Law Commission in drafting the Codes to deal with Offenses against Peace and Security and of State Responsibility. The main problem is whether or not an international community really exists. If, for example, a state commits a crime as defined by Prof. Ago, (the rapporteur of the code dealing with state responsibility) what body will determine if the state committed the crime? The proposal is to have such decisions reached by the International Court of Justice. The International Court of Justice must be given such jurisdiction, but for many years there has been no result.

The legal order as it now exists is a unilateral legal order. This is the biggest danger for the whole legal order. It stands in the way of moving toward a new legal order as you describe it in your book *Planethood*. You see it in such actions as American invasion of Grenada, the United States invasion of Panama, the Soviet invasion of Afghanistan, Czechoslovakia and so on. We must create a new psychological and political atmosphere of understanding that the prevalence of international law is not only *in* politics but *over* politics.

We can do it only with the help of public opinion. I am in touch with some writers for Izvestia who are very close to President Gorbachev. In my opinion the main thing affecting the international legal order today is the relationship between the Soviet Union and the United States. I am against the hegemony of the two superpowers. I am against a new legal order based only on the consensus between the two superpowers. But I am also against the elimination of the right of veto. I share your main ideas, dear Prof. Ferencz, but we must be very realistic and negotiate step by step.

I have some proposals for this Decade of International Law. For example, we could try to have the ILC or another body define what exactly is meant by *jus cogens*. It's supposed to be the basis of the legal order but we don't know exactly what it means. What do we really mean when we speak of "general principles of law?"

Dr Galina Shinkaretskaya: I just want to note that if you give more power to the ICJ that is a part of the existing bureaucracy. Are you just substituting a world bureaucracy for the bureaucracy in the several states? The ICJ is a pure bureaucratic mechanism which should disappear by the second millennium. *[Ed. note; she may have mis-spoken and meant ILC instead of ICJ.]*

Dr. Vladimir I. Evintov: We have a big and strong bureaucracy in the Soviet Union today. Moscow controls the entire Soviet Union. As we are now moving toward full sovereignty of the republics, including our republic, Ukraine, we will have a small bureaucracy to fight the big bureaucracy in Moscow. I would like to decentralize this international community but we cannot live without this type of bureaucracy. Bureaucracy is what manages all states.

Prof. Benjamin B. Ferencz: You have raised some interesting questions about the effectiveness of the present system and our inability to define some of our most fundamental principles in a system that doesn't work properly. These are the things we are trying to correct.

Dr. Vladimir V. Furkalo: I would like to stress the historic significance of this conference. It takes place at a time of ideological decontamination on the part of several states with regard to our position on international law. Previously we had several systems of international law. We had international law in instruments and we had international law in doctrine - either the Soviet or the United States. Gorbachev opened the way to find a common language.

Prof. Benjamin B. Ferencz: May I ask Prof. Evintov to expound a bit further on his ideas, as reflected in his book, and to elaborate on his thinking regarding what is necessary to move from a legal order of "unilateralism" to one which encompasses all human beings on this planet.

Dr. Vladimir I. Evintov: Although my book is written in Russian, in substance we all speak the same language. But do we have the same moral values which serve as the basis for the present and future international law? Until very recently, my country did not recognize the validity of certain values which were accepted in the United States, such as freedom of speech, religion and migration. Only now have we begun to introduce such a value as a free market. We must exert great efforts to build up a new foundation for the new law.

For example, British Prime Minister Thatcher believes that nuclear weapons are a value to preserve peace. But this is very dangerous. In the United States there is a strong tendency which considers the use of force as a value to impose the will of the United States. In our country the same tendency was also masked as being necessary to maintain peace. We must totally reconstruct our mentality.

The idea that international law should prevail over politics isn't so new. It was confirmed in many decisions of the International Court of Justice. But as we examine our international society today, we see that only forty states recognize the compulsory jurisdiction of the International Court of Justice. Only one of the five permanent members of the Security Council recognizes it. There is thus a very great need to strengthen the role of the International Court of Justice.

You propose the creation of an international criminal court. We must distinguish between crimes committed by the state and crimes committed by persons. The International Court of Justice is the most suitable organ to deal with crimes by states. For crimes committed by individuals, I think the idea of an International Criminal Court is very good, but I cannot see that states will agree to it because they have not yet accepted the necessary new mentality.

Prof. Benjamin B. Ferencz: You have said, correctly, that we need common norms as the basis for proceeding in a common way. In our earlier sessions, Sandra Bendfeldt, who had just returned from studying negotiating techniques at a Harvard Law School course with Prof. Roger Fisher, noted that we must list the areas of our common concern and common interests. If you consider the alternatives you may see more clearly that you have more to gain by working with your adversary rather than opposing him. We surely have a common interest in understanding each other and in agreeing upon certain minimum values which we both or all share.

The right to life, for example, is very fundamental. If the value of nuclear deterrence to preserve peace fails, and nuclear weapons are used, life has lost its value because all human life will be destroyed. Nuclear weapons may therefore work against the common value of preserving life no matter what the nationality. The point you make is valid but it must be translated into the language of law to become meaningful.

You think the International Court of Justice is the best forum for settling disputes between states. I agree completely that the jurisdiction should be expanded for all disputes which are legal in nature. But some of those disputes between states are political and not legal, and the International Court of Justice may not be the best arena to resolve such matters.

We learned at Nuremberg that crimes are committed by people and not be states. Some crimes, like genocide, can not be committed without the complicity of a state. The crimes we are concerned with - those that threaten the peace - usually require the participation of individuals functioning in high office within the state framework. That's a real problem still today.

Aggression was the first crime we dealt with at Nuremberg. Lawyers must make the definition of that crime more precise. At Nuremberg we said that the head of the German state which launched an attack against its neighbors would be held responsible. Even though he was not there to do the shooting, he organized it and was helped by other decision makers such as leading industrialists and generals, who would be held individually responsible. The state as an entity had ceased to exist as a matter of fact. As lawyers, we must think more clearly about such things.

At the last session of the General Assembly, the government of Trinidad and Tobago introduced a resolution for an international criminal court to deal with drug-trafficking and other international crimes. The United States was opposed. The USSR took a neutral position. Burma, now known as Myanmar, probably the biggest drug-trafficker in the world, was opposed to it. That brings us face to face with the type of problem mentioned by Dr. Evintov. What happens when something as sensible as a court to control drug-traffickers - where we all have a common interest - is simply not accepted by some states?

It will take greater effort before we can change the ethic and the common values. Or we may have to turn to the public and other agencies like NGO's to influence or change the decision makers who, for bureaucratic or other reasons, refuse to recognize or support the public interest.

Dr. Yuri S. Shemshouchenko: It's obvious that international law should reflect the values of humanity. At this time we are trying to clarify these values in various international instruments. But we know that many of them are not working or being enforced. That resembles the current situation in our state.

Beginning with Perestroika, we issued over 100 different legal instruments. But they are not completely enforced. The republics which are part of the Soviet Union issue their own legal instruments which sometimes contradict the general legislation of the Soviet Union. Thus there is a contradiction. The effect is that the Soviet Union is unable to make its own laws effective in some of the republics.

We still do not have a mechanism for reconciling these differences. A similar situation exists on an international scale. Thus we also need some agencies to deal with law enforcement at the international level.

In the environmental area, we are now dealing with the problem of creating an international environmental security system. It will not be effective unless there is a special international body to deal with enforcement. The USSR has proposed that an international body be created to monitor compliance with the environmental requirements. Giving jurisdiction to the International Court of Justice to deal with violations would be an additional guarantee for enforcement of environmental law.

Prof. Benjamin B. Ferencz: Your description of different laws for different regions and the inconsistencies and conflicts which arise as a result of that reminds me of the condition the United States faced in 1777 to 1787. I mention it only because we may be able to draw some lessons from it. At that time, the thirteen colonies, after declaring their independence from the British crown, became sovereign states like your new sovereign republics. They enacted their own laws, taxes, had different currencies and tariffs and militia and, not surprisingly, got into disputes.

They were working under a legal instrument called The Articles of Confederation. It was a loose association in which they didn't have a common legislature or a supreme court or any common enforcement mechanism. They had the same difficulties that you describe as existing in the Soviet Union and in the world today.

How was it handled in the United States? There was a conference, including lawyers, which set out to improve the Articles of Confederation to overcome the shortcomings. They came from all over the Eastern seaboard to meet in Philadelphia. As they tried to amend the existing system to make it workable, they discovered that it couldn't be done without a totally different approach. A new instrument and system was needed. People like Thomas Jefferson, Benjamin Franklin and others whose names have become famous, drew up the Constitution of the United States of America. What is needed now is a new constitution for the Soviet Union and the rest of the world.

The United States experience can serve as a model even if it has to be modified to meet today's needs. But we see that a legislative body was needed which would represent the people in a fair way through a Congress of two houses with the number of delegates based on population as well as statehood. A Supreme Court was added. There could be only one national army. It has worked reasonably well for 200 years , even though it was not perfect and we have had a civil war to enforce it. It was discriminatory in many ways: we had slavery, women were not allowed to vote. Not all changes could be accepted at once. But a foundation was laid which has kept the United States rich and prosperous for two centuries.

The fact that it *is* 200 years old suggests that perhaps changes are necessary to modernize it. For example, take your call for a new international environmental regime which consists of laws on the environment, guaranteed or enforced by some international body. We already have something similar in the Law of the Sea which has, in principle, already been accepted by all nations. It was a new invention by lawyers. It is a unified law which governs almost four-fifths of the surface of this planet. It has a dispute settlement mechanism - the law of the sea tribunal. Not all of the details have been worked out yet and some states are holding back on some points but there is a clear movement in the right direction. The United States has refused to accept some of the restraints since some American corporations that have the capacity to exploit the rich sea bed don't see why they should be compelled to treat their gains as "the common heritage of mankind." But, in time, that will change.

As Evintov pointed out, we may have to go to the people. We must explain that leaders, who refuse to accept a regime which almost everyone else in the world has accepted, are placing their national interest above the common interest, and that such behavior is not only immoral but also dangerous in an interdependent world. It may be difficult to convince Americans to accept something which is contrary to their own immediate interest. It would be easy to convince the Third World - which does not have to give up much because they lack the technology.

Perhaps it is up to lawyers to explain that there is a common long term interest to improve the living conditions of all people. Maybe we must also turn to educators to teach the children that the general interest is not always consistent with the immediate personal interest, which in the long run can not prevail. We see that colonialism no longer exists or is breaking down. May I ask Dr. Vladimir Furkalo, the Deputy Chief of the Department of International Relations of the Institute in the Ukraine to comment?

Dr. Vladimir V. Furkalo: The problem of law enforcement is as old as international law. We can see the problem clearly if we consider the rules of war, which is my area of expertise. Problems which can not be solved in times of peace become much more difficult in times of war.

We have no authorities which can regulate the declared international humanitarian law which is supposed to govern the activities of military forces engaged in armed conflict. Widening the authority of the International Court of Justice would be the best way to strengthen the enforcement mechanism.

International law is a balancing of interests among different states which work out the process of creating international law. Every state has its own understanding of what it means. For that reason it was so difficult to find a common language in this field. Maybe we should begin by working out a common understanding of principles or values which are genuinely shared, as Evintov recommends.

Prof. Benjamin B. Ferencz: I think everyone recognizes that it would be good if we could specify those minimum norms of international behavior which everyone shares. But that's not so easy. For example, let us take a very fundamental principle from the United Nations Charter: the Non-Use of Force. The Charter prescribes as a norm [Art.2(4)] that, in their international relations, states shall refrain from the threat or use of force. Then comes the joker - always. There's an exception. There's an "inherent right" of self defence [Art, 51]. Both seem to be perfectly valid principles and yet the two are really inconsistent. What do we as lawyers do to reconcile those differences?

Dr. Vladimir V. Furkalo: You have raised a very important problem: the definition of aggression.

Prof. Benjamin B. Ferencz: As you now, I have written a two-volume book on that. It took nations about fifty years to reach a definition. The USSR began with a simple definition: he who fires the first shot is the aggressor. Sounds clear, but it wasn't that simple. Sometimes you can't find out who fired the first shot. In the nuclear age you may never find out because you'll be dead. Can you risk waiting? The consensus definition was full of loopholes. It would not be considered aggression if the persons were seeking "self-determination" (another norm which is generally approved) or "freedom from alien domination" or a few other such exceptions. That meant that the whole definition from a legal point of view was meaningless.

Dr. Vladimir I. Evintov: As lawyers, we must insist upon a rigid definition which almost totally prohibits the use of force. We must globally prohibit the planning, production and use of nuclear arms, as well as all other means of mass destruction.

Prof. Benjamin B. Ferencz: Perhaps Galina would say that we are dreaming. Excuse me for being historical but I want to suggest that even the most sacred norms can be changed in time. For example, there was a time in our society when dueling was considered the only honorable thing to do under certain circumstances of personal insult. Adversaries would meet at dawn and each would try to put a hole in the head of the other or pierce him with a sword. That's what real gentlemen always did. Then it was made illegal by lawyers who said that it was a stupid way to settle disputes. Today, if you challenge some one to a duel in the woods in the morning he will think you're crazy! This once very fundamental value, this mark of honor, no longer exists.

The same happened to piracy and slavery. Lawyers have been able to make fundamental changes once they knew clearly what had to be done. What is needed, as Evintov says, are clear, rigid laws, without loopholes. Today, aggression means what the consensus definition specifies. Those paragraphs which say that it does not apply under certain conditions must be deleted. Those loopholes provide the excuse for aggression.

You must do the same for other conventions such as those condemning crimes against diplomats or terrorism or hostage-taking, all of which have such clauses written in for the purpose of reaching a phoney consensus. States were not really willing to give up the use of force to achieve such legitimate goals as self-determination, and freedom from alien domination.

What it means is that we must be prepared to sacrifice certain norms for the benefit of other norms which are more important in the international order. You don't have to sacrifice more than necessary. For example, in dealing with self-defense, the Charter allowed it but only under certain prescribed circumstances. It could only be used to protect against an *armed* attack and only until the Security Council could intervene.

Maybe in the nuclear age we should outlaw self-defense completely. Perhaps only the Security Council, or some other security regime which can intervene quickly and without veto, should be authorized to maintain peace. That may seem absurd at first but let me give you an example.

There was a great American hero named General Douglas MacArthur. When he defeated the Japanese after World War II, he said to them: I will have you sign a treaty which provides that you will never again be able to defend yourself. Because of your aggression, you will forever be dependent in future upon the international community to defend you. You will never be able to militarize again. Art. 9(A) of their Constitution prohibited Japan from ever having a military force that might threaten its neighbors. What was the effect?

The effect was that the Japanese spent all of their money on improving their technology and industry and took all the business away from the Americans! They got very prosperous, very rich and in fact much more powerful. The United States spent lots of the United States taxpayer's money in building arms to defend Japan, and others, wasting our resources, polluting the environment and verging on bankruptcy. Now we are urging them to defend themselves although it's not clear against what or whom - because we don't want to spend the money. Thus, as absurd as it may sound to suggest that a nation should give up its right of self-defense, we see that there may be a better way to protect the interests of a country and its people.

Once we have put into place a more effective mechanism to protect the interests of all states and people - either through a court with compulsory jurisdiction or some other agency - then it may be possible to talk seriously about world disarmament. We as lawyers must invent the necessary mechanisms.

Dr. Vladimir I. Evintov: We already have a germ of the world order in the General Assembly and the Security Council. On the political level, the world is badly managed. But, in other areas it's not so bad. For example, communications and civil aviation contain good management tools. Environmental protection may offer us our best challenge today.

In the USSR today, self-criticism is very popular. Our system of enforcement of law by independent courts is very primitive. We are now beginning to adopt the system of a law-based state which will recognize the importance of courts. I think it was very important that both the United States and the USSR took the initiative together to suggest that the International Court of Justice be given compulsory jurisdiction regarding a number of treaties. The other members of the Security Council are also considering it.

We must extend similar principles to many fields such as communications, seabed mining etc. until the common heritage concept becomes a reality. In the field of civil aviation there are good international controls. We must learn from such experiences and expand it into other spheres.

Prof. Benjamin B. Ferencz: You may be right in suggesting that we should not try to put too much under one umbrella. The United Nations Specialized Agencies are effective in dozens of areas and that nucleus of reasonably effective management can serve as a useful model for further expansion into other vital interconnected areas. Even the "common heritage" principle has already been accepted for outer-space under the prodding of lawyers.

If we can apply new and rational ideas to outer-space and the moon and the sea, maybe one day we can do it for the land. Progress doesn't move in a straight line. It goes up and it goes down and it goes around. Sometimes it is enough to discourage you but it's our duty as lawyers not to get discouraged. We must see that the general trend is a spiral upward and we must help that trend by creating useful new instruments.

Dr. Vladimir V. Furkalo: In our country we have seen that law is effective only when it responds to the level of development of certain structures either inside the country or internationally. To be too idealistic and ahead of the real conditions doesn't work. I agree with Dr. Evintov that we must try to make progress in specific areas where there is a common understanding already reached by many countries. Environment is such an example. The damage is so great that it's almost impossible to go on without change. Here is an area which is ripe for legal action.

Prof. Benjamin B. Ferencz: You are quite right in noting that law enforcement requires a certain level of development before it is ripe for acceptance and that requires time even though a more limited approach may be more readily attainable in the near future.

Dr. Vladimir I. Evintov: You have referred to the use of international police forces as a tool of law enforcement. One of our academicians, Goldanski, has argued that complete nuclear disarmament is not desirable because the United States and the USSR can, with the help of a few such weapons, become a nuclear police force for the world.

Prof. Benjamin B. Ferencz: But you, Prof. Evintov, pointed out that the assertion of power by two nations is rather undemocratic. President Roosevelt spoke of "four policemen" to enforce international law after World War II but that seems rather arrogant and I don't think it will work. Any nuclear weapons constitute a great danger. If we could have complete nuclear disarmament as well as eliminating all other weapons of mass destruction we could maintain international law and order with a much lower level of destructive capacity. Using nuclear force as now constituted seems to me to be totally irrational since most of the victims are innocent people. You cannot direct a nuclear weapon against one criminal.

One of the principles that came out of Nuremberg was that you punish only the guilty and only after a fair trial which has found them guilty beyond a reasonable doubt. To launch a nuclear weapon any place in the world is to risk killing millions of people who have committed no crime and done no wrong. Indeed they may be opposed to the policies of their government. I think we must look to enforcement in a more controlled and limited way.

Generating Political Will

Dr. Yuri S. Shemshouchenko: I think the methods of law enforcement should be improved but I don't think that enforcement in any of the fields of international law can be 100% effective. The most important thing is the political will of states— especially when concluding international treaties. Many agreements are reached by consensus but that only relates to the wording of the document. The parties often understand the articles and definitions quite differently. If, in fact, all of the states involved do not have the political will to make the instrument effective, no enforcement mechanism will help.

Whether there is the necessary political will is dependent upon the interests of the state concerned. It's the same whether one looks at the law of the sea, the air, outer-space or agreements with regard to mutual verification. Although the United States and the USSR both signed the Law of the Sea Final Act, the Sea-Bed Authority, which will deal with the allocation of resources, has not yet been created. The reason is that both countries have different approaches to the problem. In fact there was no identity of political will on the part of the Convention signers. That's the reason why the Law of the Sea is not yet effective.

The perspectives must be similar. The Soviet Union proposed that nations adopt an International Code of Ecological Ethics. It will be discussed at the upcoming conference on Environment and Development.

Prof. Benjamin B. Ferencz: Certainly you have put your finger on the crux of the problem we are dealing with - the unwillingness of states to make necessary changes in the prevailing international system. I think it's a disgrace for lawyers to prepare legal instruments by apparent consensus, knowing that they have no legal significance whatsoever. If nations can interpret agreements as they see fit to protect their own perceived interests, it's a fraud on the public. Since you will be discussing ethics, can I ask if it's ethical to pretend that law is being advanced while at the same time you are not advancing law at all because you are concealing the fact that the law is defective?

What does it take in the 21st century to generate the political will in the minds of the decision makers and bureaucrats who are today protecting their own positions and power at the expense of the people?

Dr. Vladimir V. Furkalo: I disagree a bit with my Director. Political will is very important but I don't think it's the decisive factor. Political will changes from time to time just as governments change. Political instruments should not be dependent upon such variables. They do reflect various local considerations, political, economic, social etc. Until the participants have reached such a level of development that there is some identity of such interests, enforcement and international law will be impacted.

For example, in 1977, nations adopted two Protocols Additional to the Geneva Conventions of 1949. I was a member of the Soviet delegation at the conference and I was surprised to note that both the United States and the USSR could easily agree upon most of the problems. But sometimes we couldn't find common language with other states, such as Vietnam. My explanation was that both of our nations were military superpowers and both faced similar problems.

Let me also illustrate with a problem where agreement was not possible. One of the provisions (Art. 36) required parties to consult to see whether the agreement was violated by new weapons of warfare that might be invented in the future. Have you ever heard that either the United States or the USSR lived up to that? Until other conditions are suitable, this progressive principle just won't work.

Prof. Benjamin B. Ferencz: Let me ask an educator, Dr. Rose Cooper how we can make clear to the public that they are being deceived by lawyers and diplomats who present documents as though they were binding agreements when in fact they do not represent a real meeting of the minds and will therefore not be honored.

Dr. Rose Cooper: In order to reach the people you can not talk to them about complicated laws, you must speak in a language they can understand. You must reach them through the various means of education.

You've got to start with the youngsters and move up through every hierarchy of learning. Young people must learn how laws affect us and the difference between good laws and bad laws, and the impact of laws nationally, internationally and globally.

When we talked about the environment it was clear that it is no longer a national problem - it's a global problem. Young people can grow up with the knowledge that slaws are good because they help people reach desired and necessary objectives. People become more aware of what law really means. To many people, reading about a United Nations resolution is meaningless and they don't pay any attention to it.

We must also educate those who present the commentaries on radio and TV. Educators themselves must learn about the needs for global unity of the planet if the human race is to survive. As an educator, I am a strong believer that it is possible. Education through information, communication, collaboration and cooperation is the key.

Dr. Vladimir V. Furkalo: I just want to add another illustration of my earlier point. When the Anti-Ballistics Missile (ABM) Treaty was signed, the United States was in favor of it. But, a few years later, political conditions changed and the United States came up with an interpretation that was contrary to the purposes of the treaty. Thus agreements are only effective as long as they reflect and support certain political and other relations between states.

Prof. Benjamin B. Ferencz: True, some lawyers, like Abe Sofaer, the General Counsel of the State Department, will come up with a new interpretation of the ABM treaty which supports a changed United States political policy, while other international lawyers like me will have a contrary view. But I won't let you get off simply by saying that lawyers can draw legal documents but politicians will determine policy and therefore lawyers are not to blame for what happens. If we as lawyers are unable to create a system of international law that is meaningful and workable, we must acknowledge that we are failures.

Let us assume that the political will is there and that Mr. Gorbachev and Mr. Bush and Mrs. Thatcher and whoever is the head of the new united

175

Germany and Japan and India all agree that the time has now come to create an international system that works - a system that eliminates the urgent problems of nuclear threat, nuclear waste, environmental degradation, poverty, homelessness etc. That would be the challenge to us as lawyers that we must face. If we had political leaders who were blessed with such a vision could we build a new foundation for international society so that others would not have to start from scratch?

We should not seek to create laws which are designed to control every person in every way by universal decrees. But we should have certain minimum standards that make it possible for states in different stages of development and different ethnic and cultural backgrounds to live without war while they try to overcome problems which they all have.

Let me illustrate. We have a consensus definition of aggression but it is full of loopholes. It shouldn't take lawyers long to eliminate those loopholes; we could do it together in a few hours. The same problem exists regarding the conventions to eliminate terrorism, hijacking, hostage-taking and other legal instruments theoretically designed to maintain minimum world order.

Dr. Vladimir I. Evintov: I would like to make a general objection. In our country, lawyers were ready to draw up documents expressing the stated norms, but these laws were without any force. They were artificial because they conveyed only the political will of the moment. I think it is better to weigh and to balance the interests rather than to impose laws based on the omnipotent power of the state. Only such rules will be effective.

I think the ILC and the Sixth Committee of the United Nations can work out and codify minimum norms of international behavior. We must make an inventory of such norms that already exist, including the accepted *jus cogens*, "general principles" of law etc. We must enumerate the existing rules of international behavior in every field of international relations and publish the results in many volumes. It's a big job but within the framework of the declared United Nations Decade of International Law, it's absolutely necessary.

176

The work of the main international law scholars must also be published from works of such people as Pufendorf to Benjamin Ferencz and edited under the auspices of the United Nations. The International Court of Justice, as you know, in its decisions takes into account the opinion of such publicists, so it's important for humanity.

Prof. Benjamin B. Ferencz: Everything we do here today, in the atmosphere in which we live, is artificial. I know that. The study of past works is an important tool in our effort to build something more realistic. You have suggested that we list all of the existing norms the *jus cogens* as we call it in Latin in order to confuse the public. We really don't know what they are.

We have a host of United Nations Declarations, such as the Friendly Relations Declaration, the Manila Declaration, Declarations on the Non-Use of Force etc. They all contain a lot of nice norms with a lot of nice loopholes written in for the sole purpose of making the norms meaningless or, as they say, to reach a consensus. We can put them into a book. The American Society of International Law has a project to publish a textbook on existing international law. Prof. Lori Damrosch of Columbia University, who is coordinating that project, was supposed to be with us for the conference, but had to be absent because she just gave birth to a baby. International law is also in its infancy and that baby must crawl before it can walk or start to run. We can help it along the way by doing what you suggest.

I accept it as a challenge. If we can assemble the existing documents, point to the shortcomings and suggest specific improvements we will be making a real contribution. When the political will is finally reached, international lawyers will be in a better position to move forward in a more constructive and realistic way than they can do at the moment because of limiting circumstances beyond our control.

We must remember that everything is interconnected. It's like the mechanisms of a watch. If one of the springs or gears doesn't work the watch will not keep time. Until all of the complicated mechanism needed for a peaceful world is in place we will not have created an instrument which will give us peace. But, although it may have taken years, there are fine

Swiss watches which do keep time and our job is to make the international legal system as reliable as a Swiss watch.

Enhancing Dispute Settlement by Peaceful Means

Prof. Benjamin B. Ferencz: Let's consider means of strengthening the international order by creating more effective means for the peaceful settlement of disputes. That will encompass not merely arbitration and international courts but all similar means related to it, such as fact-finding, conciliation, mediation, advisory opinions, compulsory jurisdiction of various types of courts, and whether we should deal with them on a global, regional or national level. How do we go about it?

Dr. Vladimir I. Evintov: I ask myself why we don't have a general principle of modern international law which requires self-limitation. Rather than self-help in international matters, we must rely upon international jurisdiction. We now have many systems for the resolution of conflicts or misunderstandings. For example, we have the Court of Human Rights and the Helsinki Process to deal with certain human rights complaints. In the field of disarmament, treaties between the United States and the USSR have built in certain dispute settlement mechanisms. The idea of incorporating dispute settlement arrangements within every treaty was an idea proposed by Prof. Michael Reisman (of Yale Law School). I think that would be very useful.

In all fields of possible conflict we must look to international jurisdictions to deal with it. It must be integrated into a complete system with the International Court of Justice as the main organ. The General Assembly must be able to ask the International Court of Justice for advisory opinions whenever the parties are unable to reach agreement on a legal problem affecting the legal order.

The International Court of Justice should also be engaged whenever the Security Council is unable to reach an agreement because one of its Permanent Members has exercised its veto power.

Prof. Benjamin B. Ferencz: The idea of making the International Court of Justice the supreme authority to resolve legal differences, including differences within the General Assembly and Security Council, is a very dramatic thought. It would, of course, require an amendment of the

179

International Court of Justice statute, but that's something which we as lawyers could certainly draft.

I feel that your suggestion, by giving the International Court of Justice the last word, would come close to making the International Court of Justice a legislative body. In our experience in the United States, we found that the legislative authority should rest with a non-judicial body representing the people and that the court system should be engaged only when there is a dispute regarding the interpretation of the laws laid down by the Congress. But I welcome every new thought for consideration.

It has been suggested that perhaps we should set up a special regime which would have as its sole function the interpretation and monitoring of treaties. At the moment, the International Court of Justice only has jurisdiction over such disputes as the parties willingly agree should be dealt with by the court. Suppose we had a United Nations Treaty Interpretation Section which would receive and review all treaties to see if they had ambiguous or contradictory clauses which would have to be clarified and also to monitor and report back regarding any complaints about treaty violations. It could also be used for United Nations Declarations.

Such an agency could be established within the United Nations framework as a new special organ of the General Assembly. It would be a new legal invention that might be acceptable. Would such an agency, with global authority, be helpful?

Dr. Vladimir I. Evintov: I think it's a good idea but I think it would be better if it would be an organ supported by public opinion and created outside the United Nations. It should be staffed by scholars, scientists and public figures and others who are sensitive to public interests in that particular field.

Dr. Vladimir V. Furkalo: Surely, if you come to a stalemate you should try to find a way out. But wouldn't such a new agency serve to undermine the International Court of Justice and the existing structures? Perhaps in cases where the parties are unwilling to go to the International Court of Justice it might be useful to create such a committee of scholars etc. without official status.

Dr. Yuri S. Shemshouchenko: I don't know whether it would be possible to create a new agency in addition to the International Court of Justice or the United Nations. Special Commissions might be established which are connected to the Special Agencies of the United Nations to deal with specific problems. For example, there might be a Legal Commission within the United Nations Environmental Program to deal with the legal interpretation of environmental instruments or disputes. A similar commission may be created within the Law of the Sea administration or connected with the International Sea-Bed Tribunal. Such committees composed of independent experts and writers may be effective in helping to carry out the treaties.

Prof. Benjamin B. Ferencz: The advantage of your proposal is that if you have a specialized commission presumably its simpler and the people dealing with it have a special expertise and it may be easier to get it accepted. Some of the disarmament treaties already have a built in Consultative Commission to deal with disputes.

What about a drafting committee to review and analyze all legal instruments for the purpose of noting the loopholes and inconsistencies and recommending ways to eliminate them?

In the world today we have various peaceful protesters - whether it be in China, the Baltics, the Ukraine or elsewhere. Some are threatening to secede from a union, such as in Northern Ireland. We have the principle of the non-use of force and the principle of self-determination as valid international norms. They often come into conflict and it leads to violence between people and governments. What can we, as international lawyers, suggest as a way to settle these differences by peaceful means?

Dr. Vladimir I. Evintov: Before leaving for the United States, I attended a lecture at the University of Bratislava given by a scholar from the Red Cross. I asked him whether the rules of humanitarian warfare were applicable in the conflict between Armenia and Azerbijan. He said: "No, that's an internal affair." I argued that the answer was yes because they were two sovereign states. Even though they are part of the Soviet Union, they are still sovereign states. We see the conflict between international law and politics.

I am in favor of the principle of self-determination. If the people of Lithuania don't wish to be part of the Soviet Union, I think they have a right to withdraw. But we do not live in a political vacuum and we must try to harmonize the conflicting principles.

Dr. Vladimir V. Furkalo: The question you raise is of great importance for my country at this time. From a legal point of view, it is the duty of every citizen to abide by the legal norms fixed by the laws of every country. When he violates those norms and threatens the internal stability of the country it's the right and duty of the state to enforce law and order. Even in the human rights instruments which have been generally accepted, there are provisions which state that in case of emergency some of those rights such as the right to leave, or fair trial do not apply.

Prof. Benjamin B. Ferencz: You are saying that a citizen's first duty is to obey the law of the land. On the other hand, if the laws violate emerging new norms of international behavior and human rights there is a conflict. What about the citizen's right to bear arms or to overthrow the government as we have it in the United States Constitution? If, as part of the drive for self-determination, the Ukrainians, or the American Indians or the Puerto Ricans or the Irish, wish to secede, what happens to the equally valid principle protecting the territorial integrity and political independence of states? When respected principles are in conflict, how do we find the balance which Evintov says we need?

Dr. Vladimir I. Evintov: International law must prevail over national law.

Prof. Benjamin B. Ferencz: Beautiful! Now we have two representatives from Kiev and both from the same legal institute and both called Vladimir and they completely disagree on this point. Gentlemen, how do you reconcile your differences of opinion?

Dr. Yuri S. Shemshouchenko: As Director of the Institute I respect differences of opinion. After the war, our Foreign Minister Vyschinski was addressing the United Nations General Assembly and he declared official Soviet doctrine to be that socialist law had priority over international law. Now, we have a different period of our life and we give international law priority over domestic law. At both times there were plausible reasons for the positions taken. All countries try to maintain their own sovereignty. At a recent conference I attended dealing with problems of agriculture, each nation indicated that they wanted to unite economically yet remain independent politically. That tradition influences international relations and international law. The national character of states also plays a part. In our country today, the national aspects influence the process of law making both domestically and internationally.

Prof. Benjamin B. Ferencz: If at one period there is a Vyschinski Doctrine and later there is a Gorbachev Doctrine which is the opposite, is that a rational legal system?

Dr. Vladimir I. Evintov: We are back to the point of our beginning asking whether we can have a legal system of self-limitation in the international and domestic legal order. The present community of states is not one of post-Westphalian peace based on the absolute sovereignty of nation states. An example of how states have moved toward a system of self-limitation of sovereignty is illustrated by the disarmament agreements which allow Soviet and United States inspectors on-site verification in both countries. That was unimaginable just five years ago. It is a good point of departure for the development of a new international legal order described in your excellent books.

Prof. Benjamin B. Ferencz: I was going to say "Bravo!" - even before you made reference to my books. You have correctly noted that despite the existence of a theory that the legal order is composed of independent sovereign states, that Westphalian system is breaking down. The Stalinist point of view expressed by Mr. Vyschinski has had to yield to what I think is the much wiser and more realistic view expressed today in the Soviet Union - as expressed in the speeches and statements of Mr. Gorbachev. Sovereign states are obsolete. They are yielding - they *must* yield - part of their sovereignty in order to function. The old medieval structure can not survive in a high-tech 21st century world. It's time for lawyers to synchronize the system with the times.

We face many dilemmas. A citizens duty is to obey the law, but to respect national law may mean to reject international law. We need a new philosophy, a new ethic and new awareness of the needs of our times as well as new technical means to adapt to the new realities. The legal solutions should be relatively easy. Lawyers can draw good contracts for whatever is required. The non-legal community should know that the legal gear in the watch is available to change national laws so that they also respect international needs. Then there is no inconsistency. Then the citizen can obey the law - and that is the direction in which we are moving.

It has been suggested that international dispute settlement would be enhanced if we had international fact-finding machinery in place throughout the world. Instead of waiting for a crisis and then sending someone to investigate and report - which might be too late - there should be available in different regions different experts to monitor various tense situations. For example, there could be environmental experts who could report that the Amazon forests are being burned and creating a problem that threatens others. The alarm could be sounded before it gets to a point of no return or conflict. Is that something which your Institute could recommend to your government?

Dr. Yuri S. Shemshouchenko: Yes. In the environmental field all problems are interrelated - nationally and internationally. Our nuclear accident at Czernobyl was supposed to be an internal affair but it became an international problem. Not merely because it contaminated foreign areas but because we tried to find common ways to avoid and solve such problems. That's why we invited 100 specialists from the International Atomic Energy Agency to visit us. They will make recommendations regarding nuclear contamination and its impact on health. It's a good example of how to approach these complicated problems which will require both national and international laws.

Sandra Bendfeldt: At the United Nations yesterday, I think it was Dr. Muller who noted that such instances of international cooperation always occur as a result of crises. Aren't there alternatives we can adopt without waiting for a crisis? Education is a way to raise the consciousness of people more than just writing an article in a law review. Can't we put our heads together before the crisis and try to avoid the crisis?

Prof. Benjamin B. Ferencz: Of course, you're right. All wars end and wouldn't it be smart to end them before they begin? It's too dangerous today to wait for a crisis.

Dr. Rose Cooper: Too often we get active and cooperative only after the disaster has happened. I think that rather than wait, we should put in place secure measures to be ready to intercept the crisis and avoid it. One of the main advantages of such conferences is the attempt to find something that will make us all more secure both nationally and globally.

Prof. Benjamin B. Ferencz: Thank you Rose, yes prevention is surely better than cure. In order to prevent any conflict in my household, I am asking my wife Gertrude Ferencz, who has joined us, to comment.

Gertrude Ferencz: I would like to draw attention to the fact that a new and revised edition of *Planethood* is coming out soon and will also deal with environmental problems. It is an outreach book intended to raise the consciousness of the public as part of global education.

Prof. Benjamin B. Ferencz: On that happy commercial note may I say that it is not the ultimate wisdom. Prof. Evintov also has a book coming out on this subject and so do others. There are many thoughts on the matter and it is not easy. It may require many years before our plans can be realized. But unless we know in which direction we wish to move we will never get there. The purpose of this conference is to recognize the right direction and to start moving.

Managing the Planet More Efficiently

Prof. Benjamin B. Ferencz: What we propose to discuss now are means of making international law enforcement more effective. I suggest that we need an improved management agency - like the United Nations - to deal with global problems. Can it become more democratic and an international legislative body? I'd like to discuss international arms control, which is also essential if we are to enforce international law. Finally we will discuss sanctions as a means of enforcement and social justice to encourage compliance with a revised world order. These points have already been scanned with your colleagues from Moscow but I would also welcome your views.

Dr. Yuri S. Shemshouchenko: I think there is a necessity and a desire to revise the Charter of the United Nations. There have been many changes in the world since the Charter was first adopted. Relations among states have changed significantly. The concept of new political thinking (perestroika) demands such changes.

The Specialized Agencies of the United Nations system are very important and many can be improved. For example, in 1972 the United Nations Environmental Program (UNEP) was adopted. In the period since then there hasn't been much change. There are plenty of proposals to make improvements in the field of environmental protection.

Prof. Benjamin B. Ferencz: Do you think that as part of the Decade of International Law it's time to review the Charter which is almost 50 years old?

Dr. Vladimir V. Furkalo: Every structure has its drawbacks, but I'm afraid that if you begin to meddle with it the entire structure may collapse. Instead of changing the Charter it may be better to try to improve relations inside the General Assembly and the Security Council. Again, it's a problem of political will. If there is a will there is a way. I strongly oppose the idea of revising the United Nations Charter.

Prof. Benjamin B. Ferencz: As a human being and as a lawyer, do you think it's fair to have a management structure in which only a very few of the powers have the right to veto and decide what should be done.

Dr. Vladimir V. Furkalo: The answer is yes, because the permanent members have most of the responsibility for security in the world.

Prof. Benjamin B. Ferencz: Do you think it's too much responsibility to trust it to say, India or other nations?

Dr. Vladimir V. Furkalo: Yes.

Prof. Benjamin B. Ferencz: Do you think it's fair in the General Assembly to give China with a billion people the same vote as some tiny state with a tiny population?

Dr. Vladimir V. Furkalo: Yes, under the present circumstances.

Prof. Benjamin B. Ferencz: It seems to me that any system that has two or five managing partners and nobody else has a voice in the organization is not a system that is going to be acceptable to those who do not share that power. It seems to me that a system that gives the same vote to a nation with a billion people as a nation with a hundred thousand people is not going to be accepted by those who have the larger population. If the system is not acceptable there will be resentment and there will not be a peaceful world order. Prof. Evintov, would you please comment on that.

Dr. Vladimir I. Evintov: If you wish to reform the United Nations system you must tell me the aim of the revision, what tools will you use and what will be the consequences of the revision. Regarding the inequality of the voting system may I note that in the Soviet Union there are many republics - the biggest is Russia - and there are small ones. We resolutely oppose giving the Russian republic more votes than the others. Similarly, I think that the big nations in the General Assembly can exercise their control and power through the Security Council.

The right of veto is a right and a duty. I agree that the notion of permanent members or great powers is based upon old imperialistic approaches. But we must be realistic. If there were no veto right, it might turn to anarchy.

The purpose of United Nations reform must be to enrich the United Nations structure through public advisory opinions relayed quickly by such private councils as I had suggested, without diminishing the role of the International Court of Justice. We can use a specialized agency to monitor all of the emerging conflicts. The superpowers must participate with all of their resources in such an agency.

Dr. Vladimir V. Furkalo: Do you feel a need also to revise the American constitution? I believe that not all Americans are happy with it but the system of checks and balances helps to solve all problems despite the fact that it's more than 200 years old. The Soviet Constitution adopted in 1936 during Stalin's time is much more democratic than the constitution adopted by Brezhnev in 1977. Yet plenty of atrocities took place under Stalin.

Dr. Yuri S. Shemshouchenko: We shouldn't be blind and we should recognize that the United Nations Charter was adopted more than 40 years ago, when the world was completely different than today. Now that times have changed I think we should be introducing more democratic ideas into the Charter. Dr. Evintov's proposal suits me more than the one by Furkalo.

Prof. Benjamin B. Ferencz: I like what your Director said about changing the Charter to keep pace with changing times. Let me answer Mr. Furkalo's question about the United States constitution. That has also changed. We immediately added a Bill of Rights and have made more than twenty amendments and are constantly considering others.

Law is not a static thing. It must keep changing. In our society, we were helped because we had a Supreme Court to interpret the constitution and give meaning to such vague phrases as "due process." The Court was able to take into account the need to balance conflicting interests along lines that Evintov was suggesting.

If we accept the proposition that society changes and that law, to be effective, must keep pace with the changes, then it would follow that if the Soviet Union is changing for whatever reason then there must be lawyers to help guide the direction of legal change as well. If we are talking about planetary management and have an institution which is over 40 years old trying to guide a very changed world, isn't it our duty as lawyers to suggest changes in those areas where the institution obviously doesn't work well? If we can balance the need for improvement as against the needs for stability - which is also an important consideration - and find some acceptable ground for compromise shouldn't we do that? Dr. Muller told us that we must be ahead of our time and not merely trying to catch up with the lag.

Sandra Bendfeldt: Muller mentioned that the era of lawyers may be past as well as the era of economists. Perhaps because they were not able to keep pace with what was required.

Prof. Benjamin B. Ferencz: Lawyers are essentially conservative. They take the law as they find it and try to adhere to it and change it only when we must. Robert Muller, also trained in law, says that what the lawyers are talking about today is relative nonsense. He sees the environmental catastrophe that looms before us and he thinks lawyers and others should be focusing on that cataclysmic change that now threatens to destroy the planet. He feels we must think ahead and in cosmic terms. He is, I think, right in noting that if we recognized an imminent threat from some extraterrestrial force we would immediately reach agreement on managing this planet for maximum efficiency.

Sandra Bendfeldt: Maybe we can have some brainstorming of options to get around these problems about which we seem to have differences. We must discuss how we can reach common goals such as equal rights.

Dr. Vladimir V. Furkalo: I think we already have equality at the level of the General Assembly. The veto right in the Council is created primarily for crisis situations.

Prof. Benjamin B. Ferencz: Sandra has asked me to review for our colleagues from Kiev the Binding Triad theory which was already discussed with the lawyers from Moscow. Richard Hudson, who is a leading proponent of that theory would convert the Assembly into a legislative body with resolutions that would become binding law, providing they meet three different tests: 1 - A majority, or some other ratio of the present membership. 2 - A vote based on population and 3 - Based on wealth as measured by Gross National Product or size of contribution to the United Nations budget. Only when all three votes are in favor, would the resolution become binding law. Paul Szasz has suggested variations which you will find in the minutes.

The Security Council would also be revised to eliminate the arrogance of power, as I call it, and spread that power over a broader base. At the same time, because everything is linked, we would have to eliminate all nuclear weapons and create an international military force which would be an international civil service only adequate to maintain international law and order among disarmed states.

That kind of a structure would entail a major reform of the United Nations Charter and organization. It can only be done when sovereign states are ready to yield part of their sovereignty because they recognize that, in the long run, they will save money on the arms race, increase their security and be more democratic. This will all have to be discussed at a new "Dumbarton Oaks Conference."

In the arms control field we discussed the need for "transparency" and we considered new theories of security based on showing your neighbor that you do not threaten him. The idea of defensive defense is being debated. Dietrich Fischer and Randall Forsberg are among the United States pioneers in that field. We also saw, in the INF treaty, that verification is possible. Is such a rational approach possible? Rose Cooper says that no one around this table could be against it, but there are many others who don't think it's a good idea.

Dr. Vladimir I. Evintov: Let me explain why I am for it. International law, as illustrated by the Helsinki Final Act, now recognizes the need for confidence-building measures. We saw it in the introduction of "hot-lines" between our two governments, joint space efforts of our cosmonauts, and on-site verification of nuclear blasts. I think it was a revolution in international relations and the international law of security. Such measures are expanding in other domains such as human rights.

Dr. Vladimir V. Furkalo: The era of openness arose in 1972 with the ABM Treaty which allowed verification by "national technical means." That began the "open skies doctrine". It was the legalization of spying.

Dr. Yuri S. Shemshouchenko: That was the beginning of a new era even if it hasn't worked very well up to now.

Social Justice and Peace

Prof. Benjamin B. Ferencz: In our earlier sessions, we noted that there can be no peace without justice and no justice without peace. If people feel that they are victims of injustice they will rebel. If we spend all of our money on armaments we will not have the resources to help people meet their legitimate needs for sustenance of body and mind.

Throughout this planet, there are millions of people who are starving, who have no drinking water and who are homeless and illiterate. Six million children die every year in a new Holocaust because they lack the few pennies worth of salts to prevent their dehydration and dysentery.There are others who are rich, who waste and pollute the resources of the planet and who have a much higher life expectancy. Those human beings who have the means to help should be ashamed if they don't try to help correct such injustices and social inequities.

International law has helped to eliminate such a world plague as malaria. Let us consider how we, as lawyers, can help to eliminate some of the many injustices which exist today throughout the global community?

Dr. Vladimir I. Evintov: Solutions can best be found via economic and political action. There must be the political will to restructure the system of social welfare by transfers from some of the richest states. The role for lawyers is limited. The richest states must be willing to renounce the re-payment of certain debts from the poorest countries and be willing to pro-vide necessary assistance.

The immediate problem is where the necessary resources are to come from. I believe they can be found by conversion from the military to civil-ian use. Here lawyers can be helpful by proposing a new centralized sys-tem which takes into account the successes in the field of demilitarization and decide how and where the savings are to be allocated. A new organi-zation might be needed to serve as a link between those who need help and those who provide it.

Prof. Benjamin B. Ferencz: When Mr. Gorbachev addressed the United Nations, he recognized that conversion from military to peaceful production was a complicated problem and he offered to cooperate with other nations in coping with it most effectively. The United States paid scant attention to it, but now it is getting more acute because of economic pressures on the United States caused by the heavy burden of the arms budget and rising social needs at home. Americans are already beginning to argue about what to do with the "peace dividend." You have raised the same problem on the international scene.

You have suggested that the developed world cancel the debt burden which is carried by non-developed states which have been forced to bor-row at high interest rates. Much of their production does not go to improve the condition of their people but to pay interest to rich foreign banks. In many instances, the very poor are thus supporting the rich. It is surely an injustice which we must address and redress.

The reality, in both the United States and I'm sure in the USSR, is that the military bureaucracy wants to reduce as little as possible rather than as much as possible. The size of any saving is limited and the demand for the saving is enormous. What can lawyers do to reconcile such differ-ences in a just and socially constructive way?

Dr. Yuri S. Shemshouchenko: Since we are considering what is fundamentally an economic problem it is very important that we try to create a new economic order in the world. Some steps are already being taken in that direction. There is a role for legal specialists as can be seen from the many international legal instruments which have already been adopted with regard to this problem.

At the same time, it must be noted that most of these instruments have not been transferred into the internal domestic legal systems. The legal instruments are recommendations only and they are not put into practice. Although they are important, they are largely ignored. Jurists must work to convert the recommendations in this field into domestic law in order to make them a reality.

Prof. Benjamin B. Ferencz: The United Nations has for years discussed the New International Economic Order. The net result was really nothing. Most nations that have the resources don't want anyone else to tell them what to do with them. Some of them are very generous. I think the United States is usually very generous but not in accepting instructions from some other state or the United Nations.

Very often, United States allocations are used for political purposes which may not always help the people. From a legal point of view that's a bit absurd. If we don't agree with the political ideology of the leader of country A, for example, we punish the people of country A and they become convinced that the leader is right in fighting the United States as an enemy of the people - and that keeps him in power.

We seem to have as a legal principle that every nation has sovereignty over the natural resources on or in its own territory. It can do with such resources whatever it sees fit. Is that a rational principle of management in a global society? Is there a better way, and can lawyers contribute to understanding and creating it?

Dr. Vladimir V. Furkalo: The answer is simple. The right of property, both private and national is sacred. Except for a few special cases, like the treasures of the seabed, I believe that most natural resources should

194

belong to the country. I may want your shirt and from my point of view I would be justified in asking to share it, but from your point of view you would oppose it.

Prof. Benjamin B. Ferencz: That's very interesting. I am listening to a distinguished researcher from the Institute of State and Law in the Ukraine, a member of the USSR, saying "The right of property is sacred." Karl Marx would turn over in his grave! Let me ask another old-time communist for his views. Yuri, do you also think the right of property is sacred?

Dr. Yuri S. Shemshouchenko: Surely not. Let me talk about national jurisdiction over the seabed and the principle of "common heritage of mankind." For the immediate future, I believe that the use of natural resources should remain under the jurisdiction of the state. But resources which are outside the territory of the state could be considered "common heritage" of mankind. The concept is very useful and the United Nations can play a very effective role in defining it and putting it into effect.

There is some tendency to consider property which is under national jurisdiction to be subject to international jurisdiction. For example, the tropical forests of the Amazon are of great significance for all mankind (since it provides oxygen for the planet) and there is some inclination to regard it as a sort of natural preserve for humanity. There are special lists of such territories which are considered part of the "common heritage." Those states which signed the Paris Convention should not arbitrarily use these resources. I believe that the tendency to take the common interests of mankind into account is a good tendency.

Prof. Benjamin B. Ferencz: I'm glad to see you thinking globally on environmental problems - at least regarding areas that are in the common domain or have a global impact. Let me see how far you are ready to go.

Let us suppose that a country like the United States produces a lot of grain and the people in the Soviet Union need that grain in order to live. Should the farmers in Kansas be entitled under international law to say that they will not sell grain to the Soviet Union, knowing that millions of people may die as a result? Country A, exercising legal control over its natural resources, is able to cause the death of large numbers of people in country B. Another variation: OPEC countries, which control the oil resources, decide that they won't sell to the United States. The result is that millions in the United States become unemployed or may freeze to death for lack of fuel. Are we, as international lawyers, prepared to say "that's OK, we respect their national sovereignty and their right to exercise control over their natural resources?"

Dr. Yuri S. Shemshouchenko: The problem is one of new political thinking. It should be solved on a bilateral basis.

Prof. Benjamin B. Ferencz: Can you solve the problem of rain-forests bilaterally? There are many resources which have a global impact such as air, food and water. If you are to have rational management of resources, you need some regime to allocate certain minimums which are essential to human life.

Can we not as lawyers recognize and define certain minimum human needs such as medical care, sustenance, education, housing etc. which are vital for human dignity and which therefore must be managed in a global way? Are these not human entitlements which supercede the right of a nation state which, by pure chance, happens to be blessed with a super-abundance of certain minerals or other r atural assets?

Why should my children have more than they can eat while children in Africa must die of starvation? I don't want to sound like Karl Marx while those from the Soviet Union are arguing for capitalism. What an interesting twist.

Dr. Vladimir V. Furkalo: Shall we approach the problem from a political, ethical or legal point of view? We are trained to solve ethical problems by means of law. If law protects the right of private property, the owner can do with it whatever he wishes - even destroy it. If we shift away from a legal approach to a political one I believe we could get lost.

Prof. Benjamin B. Ferencz: I believe that the object of law is to help create an ethical society. I believe that is in the common interest or else law would not be accepted. People will rebel against it. Ethics and justice are related.

Dr. Vladimir V. Furkalo: History shows us that rich nations have enough political will and ethics to share their excess wealth with others.

Prof. Benjamin B. Ferencz: Sharing isn't working so well as long as millions of people are still dying of starvation. I think there is need for a change in the management of the limited resources on this planet.

Dr. Vladimir V. Furkalo: We could create a legal mechanism to accumulate stockpiles of surplus resources to help nations in time of need.

Prof. Benjamin B. Ferencz: Let me give you an example. After World War II, Germany had the problem of what to do with a person whose house was totally destroyed by a bomb, but his neighbors house was undamaged. One might say that's just a matter of luck and too bad. They didn't do that. They set up a system to equalize the burdens by taxing the houses that were standing and gave the money to the neighbor to help rebuild his house. (I am simplifying for clarity.) They used law to set up a system of burden sharing.

We have a similar situation in the world today. Half the world is bombed out while the other half has its house still standing. Can we as lawyers draft an equalization of burdens law? Surely, the one who has to give up something may resist such a law, but the resistance will be limited if it is made clear that the law is fair and that protection against catastrophe, like insurance, is good for everybody.

Gertrude Ferencz: We all accept the burden of taxation on a national level which is a means of taking care of the needs of everyone. Isn't it possible to envision a form of international taxation for the world's good?

Prof. Benjamin B. Ferencz: A good legal suggestion from my wife. I'm glad to see that living with a lawyer for fifty years, and being the mother of two lawyers, has had an impact even though she interjects that it is a humanitarian approach.

Dealing with Outlaw Nations: The Problem of Sanctions

Prof. Benjamin B. Ferencz: When, earlier in the conference, we discussed enforcement of international law, we said that we must have international control of armaments. There will always be someone in the international community that will not be willing to accept any of the reasonable rules which we as lawyers can devise and which may be accepted by other states. They will simply refuse to be concerned or do anything if others starve or freeze. They reject whatever equalization laws are passed by the international community. How do we deal with outlaw nations?

Do we need an international military force of sufficient size to coerce other sovereign states and can the United Nations handle it? Can economic sanctions be so organized that they will really work? Can humanitarian laws cope adequately with the armed conflicts which will ensue?

Sandra Bendfeldt: These things cannot simply be enacted and accepted. Change is an evolutionary process and we must create the new "myths" which will replace the old "myths" which prevent change. Only through planetary education can we move forward. We noted that regional alliances are now forming that will be stronger than individual states. The regional group will be able to exert more pressure on the lawless state than some international decree.

Prof. Benjamin B. Ferencz: You are right in your reference to "myths." We live by symbols. One of the most ridiculous that I see very often is the arrival of a head of state in a foreign land. He is usually greeted by the traditional 21-gun salute after he has reviewed a line of human robots standing rigidly at attention in resplendent military uniforms with sabers drawn. It is a glorification of medieval militarism. In order to end the myth that this is the highest form of honor and glory, I might suggest that the guns be aimed at the visitor! At least we could make the glorification of war illegal. Wouldn't it be a better and more useful symbol to have visitors greeted by young children carrying flowers and singing songs of peace and welcome?

Our statues, our newspapers and our television glorify war and the use of force and violence. Sandra has interjected that monuments, as she saw them in the Soviet Union, can also be used as a reminder of how horrible war can be. I agree that countries which have suffered most heavily by recent wars, like the Soviet Union, are more inclined to note the pathos and tragedy of war than it's glories. Still, many TV programs are based on killing somebody to show what a big hero you are. The macho Rambo image is still a powerful symbol in our society and it is a symbol not for peace but for war.

After the first world war, diplomats concluded that the economic weapon of sanctions against the law-breaking state would be effective to maintain peace. The reality was different. When, for example, Haille Selassie of Ethiopia appealed to the League that his country had been a victim of aggression by Italy and demanded sanctions, including halting oil shipment for Mussolini's tanks, the British and French - for their own political reasons - refused to go along with the boycott.

Today we have the capacity through satellite monitoring of all of the earth's resources to impose effective sanctions. It's up to lawyers to see that appropriate laws are passed internationally and nationally to assert the required export and import controls. We have models already on the books - for example the laws which prohibit the export of high-technology or nuclear materials.

Dr. Yuri S. Shemshouchenko: Economic sanctions can be affective if they are based on economic treaties between countries. If the contract is not fulfilled, the offender is punished. But if economic sanctions are used as a political instrument, I believe that is wrong and inhuman. We had an experience recently when we imposed sanctions against Lithuania by cutting off oil and gas supplies to the people.

Prof. Benjamin B. Ferencz: I appreciate your humanitarian concern which is very relevant. Sanctions must be directed against the guilty party only and not penalize the innocent. That's one of the difficulties with economic sanctions based on the state system. You may object to the sovereign so you punish the people. It's an inhuman approach to the problem.

Dr. Vladimir I. Evintov: In the present system of sovereign states there are certain principles which still apply. For example, there is a principle which calls for cooperation in the solution of common problems without the use of force. These international laws and principles must be respected and, if necessary, enforced by economic sanctions.

Dr. Vladimir V. Furkalo: I agree completely with the Chief of our delegation. Our history shows, for example in the case of South Africa, that economic sanctions don't work. If they are imposed too rigidly that stimulates the impulse of the target state to develop its own or other resources. Reprisals are an effective way in war to make your enemy stop doing what he is doing, but it creates great hardships and in the Additional Protocols to the Geneva Convention that right is restricted. Sanctions in peacetime and sanctions in wartime are quite different but generally speaking, I am against this method of carrying on international relations.

Prof. Benjamin B. Ferencz: We see, in conclusion, that creating a peaceful world is not an easy job. There are difficulties which are legal, political, psychological, educational, and moral which must all be resolved. We cannot expect solutions in a short period of time but we should not be discouraged. Progress is being made in many areas which we have not been able to explore in this brief period.

What we have started is a process - a process in which we challenge our own theories and our own systems to seek means of improving the conditions under which this planet lives. If we can continue this process in an open and frank dialogue, as we have done, we can as lawyers and human beings reach out for a better world system and one of these days we are bound to find it.

Thank you all very much. It has been a pleasure having you with us. Our conference is closed.

World Security for the 21st Century

Bibliography

Al-Ebraheem, Hassan Ali. Kuwait and the Gulf: Small States and the International System. Washington, D.C.: Center for Contemporary Arab Studies; 1984. 117 p.; ISBN: 0-932568-08-4.

Alimov, Yuri. The Rise and Growth of the Non-Aligned Movement. Moscow: Progress Press; 1987. 229 p. Note: Translated from Russian.

Anand, Ram Prakash. Confrontation or Cooperation?: International Law and the Developing Countries. Dordrecht, Netherlands; Boston, Mass.: Martiunus Nijhoff; 1987. xii, 274 p.; ISBN: 90-247-3438-X.

Andemicael, Berhanykun, editor. Regionalism and the United Nations. Alpen aan den Rijn, The Netherlands; Dobbs Ferry,New York, U.S.A.: Sijthoff and Noordhoff; Oceana Publications, Inc.; 1979. xx, 603 p. (Published for the United Nations Institute for Training and Research, UNITAR.); ISBN: 0-379-00591-3.

Arangio-Ruiz, Gaetano. The United Nations Declaration on Friendly Relations and the system of the sources of international law: with an appendix on the concept of international law and the theory of international organization. Alphen aan den Rijn,Netherlands; Germantown, Md.: Sijthoff and Noordhoff; 1979.xiii, 341 p.

Artis, Michaeland Ostry, Sylvia. International Economic Policy Coordination. London; New York: Routledge Kegan Paul; 1986. vi, 89 p. (Chatham House Papers; Royal Institute of International Affairs; no. 30); ISBN: 0-7102-0892-8.

Barratta, Joseph P., Compiler. Strenghthening the United Nations: A Bibliography on U.N. Reform and World Federalism. Westport, Conn.: Greenwood Press; 1987; ISBN: 0-313-25840-6.A partially annotated bibliography of 2874 books and articles and a listing of 96 organizations dealing with U.N. reform and world federalism.

Bassiouni, M. Cherif. A Draft International Criminal Code and Draft Statute for an International Criminal Tribunal. 2nd,rev. ed. Dordrecht, Netherlands; Boston, Mass.: M. Nijhoff;Note: includes bibliography, pp. 271-353.

Bassiouni, M. Cherif. International Crimes: Digest/Index of International Instruments, 1815-1985. New York: Oceana Publications; 1986: 301. 2 vol.; ISBN: 0-379-20138-0 (v.1); 0-379- 20139-9 (v.2).

Bassiouni, M. Cherif. International Extradition: U.S. Law and Practice. 2nd. ed. Dobbs Ferry, New York: Oceana Publications; 1983-. 2 binders. (International Law Looseleaf Services); ISBN: 0-379-20746.

Basso, Lelio, editor ((International Foundation for the Rights and Liberation of Peoples)). Theory and Practice of Liberation at the End of the XXth Century. Brussels, Belgium: Establissements Emile Bruylant; 1988. 615 p.

Bernhardt, Rudolf, Director of the Project under the Auspices of the Max Planck Institute. Encyclopedia of Public International Law. New York: North-Holland Publishing Co.;   1981-87; ISBN: 0- 444-86140-8. Twelve-volume encyclopedia containing approximately 1100 articles.

Bertrand, Maurice, The Third Generation World Organization.Dordrecht; Boston; London: Martinus Nijhoff; 1989. xiii, 217p.; ISBN: 0-7923-0382-2. A theory of the possibilities for peace in recent changes in international relations, and how a new World Constitution can be structured.

Blaustein, Albert and Flanz, Gisbert. Constitutions of the Countries of the World. Dobbs Ferry, New York: Oceana Publications; 1971--with current supplements. 17 binders and supplement binder. (International Law Looseleaf Services);ISBN: 0-379-00467-4.

Blaustein, Albert. Constitutions of Dependencies and Special Sovereignties. Dobbs Ferry, New York: Oceana Publications;1975-- with current supplements. 6 binders. (International Law Looseleaf Services); ISBN: 0-379-00278-7.

Blechman, Barry M., editor. Global Security: a Review of Strategic and Economic Issues. Boulder: Westview; 1987. xiv, 258 p.; ISBN: 0-8133-0480-6.

Blishchenko, Igor Pavlovich and Zhdanov, N. Terrorism and International Law. Moscow: Progress Press; 1984. 286 p.Note: Translated from the Russian.

Bogomolov, Oleg T. and Vakhreameyev, A. The Socialist Community's Effort for Peace and Disarmament. Moscow: Nauka; 1984. 93 p.(International Peace and Disarmament Series; Scientific Research Council on Peace and Disarmament; no. 15).

Bonkovsky, Frederick O. International Norms and National Policy. Grand Rapids, Mich.: William B. Eerdmans; 1980. xiii, 220 p.

Borgese, Elisabeth Mann. The Future of the Oceans: A Report to the Club of Rome. Montreal: Harvest House; 1986. xvi, 144 p.

Boswell, Terry, and Bergesen, Albert, editors. America's Changing Role in the World-System. New York: Praeger; 1987. xii 300 p.; ISBN: 0-275-92417-3. supplement binder. (International Law Looseleaf Services); ISBN: 0-379-00467-4.

Boyle, Francis Anthony. Defending Civil Resistance Under International Law. Dobbs Ferry, New York: Transnational Publishers, Inc.; 1987. xxii, 378 p.; ISBN: 0-941320-43-X.Note: Preface by Alex Miller; foreword by Sean MacBride,S.C.; introduction by Richard Falk.

Boyle, Francis Anthony. World Politics and International Law. Durham, North Carolina: Duke University Press; 1985. xi, 366 p. (Duke Press Policy Studies); ISBN: 0-8223-0609-3.

Brogan, Patrick. The Fighting Never Stopped: A Comprehensive Guide to World Conflict Since 1945. 1st American ed. New York: Random House (Vintage Books); 1990. xx, 603 p.; ISBN:0- 679-72033-2.
Note: Originally published in 1989 in Great Britain by Bloomsbury Publishing, Ltd. under the title World Conflicts.A guide to all of the major conflicts unresolved as

of the late 1980's, containing short histories and evaluations of the current status of each conflict, it can be used as a convenient factual reference work for such topics as world order studies, war prevention, and war termination.

Brownlie, Ian. Principles of Public International Law. 4th ed. Oxford: Clarendon Press; 1990.

Buergenthal, Thomas, editor. Contemporary Issues in International Law: Essays in Honor of Louis B. Sohn. Kehl, West Germany, and Arlington, Va.: N.P. Engel; 1984. viii, 571 p.; ISBN:3-88357-040-0.

Buergenthal, Thomas and Norris, Robert. Human Rights: the Inter-American System. Dobbs Ferry, New York: Oceana Publications;1982--with current supplements. 3 binders. (International Law Looseleaf Services); ISBN: 0-379-20723-0.

Bull, Hedley and Watson, Adam, editors. The Expansion of International Society. Oxford, England: Clarendon Press;1984. xi, 479 p.; ISBN: 0-16-821942-3.

Bush, W.M. Antarctica and International Law: A Collection of Inter-state and National Documents. London; Rome; and New York: Oceana Publications, Inc.; 1982-1988. 3 volumes.

Butler, William E., compiler, translator, and author of introductory materials. Collected Legislation of the USSR and the Constituent Union Republics: Legislation and Constitutions. Dobbs Ferry, New York: Oceana Publications; 1978-1985. 7 binders. (International Law Looseleaf Services); ISBN: 0-20450-9.

Butler, William Elliot, compiler and editor. The USSR, Eastern Europe and the Development of the Law of the Sea. Dobbs Ferry, New York: Oceana Publications; 1983--with current supplements. 2 binders. (International Law Looseleaf Services); ISBN: 0-379-20851-2.

Butler, William E., editor. International Law and the International System. Dordrecht; Boston; and Lancaster: Martinus Nijhoff Publishers; 1987. 208 p. Note: Record of a 1986 symposium of British and Soviet scholars.

BIBLIOGRAPHY

Butler, William E., editor. The Non-Use of Force in International Law. Dordrecht; Boston; and London: Martinus Nijhoff Publishers; 1989. 250 p.; ISBN: 0-7923-0293-1. Note: Revised versions of papers presented at the second Anglo-Soviet Symposium on Public International Law at the Institute of State and Law, USSR Academy Sciences at Moscow, May 21-24, 1988. 3 essays on the principle of non-use of force; 7 on the role of international institutions; 4 on self-defense; and 2 on economic power.

Carter, Barry E. International Economic Sanctions: Improving the Haphazard U.S. Legal Regime. Cambridge: Cambridge University Press; 1988. xiv, 290 p.; ISBN: 0-521-34258-9.

Cassesse. Antonio and Weiler, Joseph H.H., editors. Change and Stability in International Law-Making. West Berlin; New York: W. de Gruyter; 1988. x, 214 p. (Series A, Law no. 9); ISBN: 3-11- 011494-1; 0-89925-420-9. Note: Based on the Proceedings of Two International Colloquia held at the European University Institute, Florence.

Cassesse, Antonio. International Law in a Divided World. Oxford, England: Clarendon Press; 1986. xv, 429 p.; ISBN 0-19- 87619-4-5.

Cassesse, Antonio. Violence and Law in the Modern Age. S.J.K. Greenleaves, translator. Princeton, New Jersey: Princeton University Press; 1988. 194 p.; ISBN: 0-7456-0491-9.

Catudal, Honore M. Soviet Nuclear Strategy from Stalin to Gorbachev: A Revolution in Soviet Military and Political Thinking. Berlin: Spitz; 1988. 413 p. (Militarpolitik und Rustungsbegrenzung; 6); ISBN: 3-87061-272-X.

Chan, Stephen. Issues in International Relations: a View from Africa. London: MacMillan Publishers; 1987. viii, 206 p.;ISBN: 0-333-44102-8.

Chayes, Abram. The Cuban Missile Crisis: International Crises and the Role of the Law. Lanham: University Press of America; 1987. xi, 157 p.; ISBN: 0-8191-6717-7.

Chen, Lung-chu. An Introduction to Contemporary International Law: A Policy-Oriented Perspective. New Haven and London:Yale University Press; 1989. 450 p.; ISBN: 0-300-03910-7.

Clark, Grenville, and Sohn, Louis B, World Peace through World Law; Two Alternative Plans. 3rd, enlarged ed. Cambridge,Mass.: Harvard University Press; 1966. iv, 535 p.

Cohen, Sheldon M. Arms and Judgement: Law, Morality, and the Conduct of War in the Twentieth Century. Boulder; San Francisco; and London: Westview Press; 1989. xiii, 226 p.

Damaska, Mirjan R. The Faces of Justice and State Authority: A Comparative Approach to the Legal Process. New Haven and London: Yale University Press; 1986. xi, 247 p.

D'Amato, Anthony. International Law: Process and Prospect. Dobbs Ferry, New York: Transnational; 1986. vi, 250 p.; ISBN: 0- 941320-35-9.

Damrosch, Lori Fisler, editor. The International Court of Justice at a Crossroads. Dobbs Ferry, New York: Transnational Publishers, Inc.; 1987. xxviii, 511 p. Note: Published under the auspices of the American Society of International Law.

Day, Alan J., editor. Peace Movements of the World. Harlow:Longman; 1986. viii, 398 p. (Keesing's Reference Publications); ISBN: 0-582-90268-1. Note: Reference.

Dean, Jonathan. Meeting Gorbachev's Challenge: How to Build Down the NATO-Warsaw Pact Confrontation. New York: St. Martin's Press; 1989. 450 p.

Deger, Saadet. Military Expenditure in Third World Countries: the Economic Effects. London, England and Boston, Mass.: Routledge and Kegan Paul; 1986. xv, 288 p. (International Library of Economics); ISBN: 0-7102-0304-7.

BIBLIOGRAPHY

Detter De Lupis, Ingrid. The Concept of International Law. Stockholm: Norstedts Forlag; 1987. 145 p.; ISBN: 91-1-867652- X.

Detter De Lupis, Ingrid. International Law and the Independent State. 2nd ed. Brookfeild, Vermont: Gower Publishing Co.; 1987. xxvi, 252 p.

Deutsch, Morton. Distributive Justice: Social- Psychological Perspective. New Haven, Conn. and London: Yale University Press; 1985; ISBN: 0-300-03290-0.

Dhokalia, R.P. The Codification of Public International Law. Manchester, U.K.; Dobbs Ferry. New York: Manchester University Press; Oceana Publications, Inc.; 1970. xiv, 367 p.

Dilloway, James. Is World Order Evolving?: An Adventure into Human Potential. Oxford, England; New York: Pergamon Press; 1986. xvi, 261 p. (Systems science and world order library); ISBN: 0-08- 033378-8.

Dinstein, Yoram. War, Aggression and Self-Defense. Cambridge: Grotius Publications Limited; 1988. xxx, 292 p.; ISBN: 0-949009 15-6.

Durante, Francesco. Western Europe and the Development of the Law of the Sea: National Legislation. Dobbs Ferry, New York: Oceana Publications; 1979-. 4 binders. (International Law Looseleaf Services); ISBN:0-379-20286-7. Note: Set now closed; updated by Simmonds' New Directions in the Law of the Sea.

Edwards, A.J.C. Nuclear Weapons, the Balance of Terror, the Quest for Peace. Bassingstoke, England: Macmillan; 1986. xvii, 275 p.; ISBN: 0-333-39564-6.

Efimov, Gennadii K. UN Charter as an Instrument of Peace. Moscow: Nauka Publishers; 1986. 130 p. (International Peace and Disarmament Series; no. 39.)

Elagab, Omer Yousif. The Legality of Non-Forcible Counter- Measures in International Law. Oxford, England: Clarendon Press; 1988. xxix, 255 p. (Oxford Monographs in International Law); ISBN: 0-19-825590-X.

Elias, Taslim Olawale. The International Court of Justice and Some Contemporary Problems: Essays on International Law. The Publishers; 1983. ix, 374 p. (Legal Aspects of International Organizations); ISBN: 90-247-2921-1.

Falk, Richard; Kratochwil, Fredrich; and Mendlovitz, Saul H.,editors. International Law: a contemporary perspective. Boulder, Colorado: Westview Press; 1985. xiii, 702 p. (Studies on a just world order; no. 2); ISBN: 0-66531-241-9.

Falk, Richard; Kim, Samuel S.; and Menovitz, Saul H., editors.Toward a Just World Order. Boulder, Colorado; Westview Press;(1982). x, 652 p. (Studies on a just world order; vol. 1); ISBN: 0-86531-242-7.

Fawcett, James E.S. Law and Power in International Relations. London: Faber and Faber; 1982. 140 p. (Studies in International Politics); ISBN: 0-571-10537-8.

Ferencz, Benjamin B. A Common Sense Guide to World Peace. London; New York: Oceana Publications; 1985: xvi, 112 p.; ISBN:0-379-20797-4. Note: Includes bibliography. Introduction by Louis B. Sohn.

Ferencz, Benjamin B. Defining International Aggression; The Search for World Peace: a Documentary History and Analysis. Dobbs Ferry, New York: Oceana Publications; 1975. 2 volumes. ISBN:0-379-00271-X.

Ferencz, Benjamin B. An International Criminal Court: A StepToward World Peace: a documentary history and analysis. London and New York: Oceana Publications, Inc.; 1980. 2 volumes; ISBN: 0- 379-20390-1.

Ferencz, Benjamin B. in cooperation with Ken Keyes Jr. Planethood: The Key to Your Survival and Prosperity. Coos Bay, Oregon: Vision Books; 1988. 188 p.; ISBN: 0-915972-14-X.

Ferencz. Benjamin B. Enforcing International Law, a Way to World Peace: a Documentary History and Analysis. London; New York: Oceana Publications; 1983: 1700. 2 vol. ISBN: 0-379-12148-4.

Fischer, Dietrich; Nolte, Wilhelm; Oberg, Jan; and Transnational Foundation for Peace and Future Research. Winning Peace: Strategies and Ethics for a Nuclear-free World. New York; Philadelphia; London: Crane, Russak and Co.; Taylor and Francis; Taylor and Francis Ltd.; 1989. xi, 272 p.; ISBN: 0-8848-1574-8; 0-8848-1575-6 (pbk).

Fisher, Roger. Improving Compliance with International Law. Charlottesville, Virginia: University Press of Virginia; 1981. 370 p. (Procedural Aspects of International Law Series; 14); ISBN: 0-8139-0859-0.

Fisher, Roger and Ury, William. Getting to Yes: Negotiating Agreement Without Giving In. New York: Penguin Books; 1983. xiii, 161 p. Note: Originally published by Houghton Mifflin in Boston, 1981.

Forsythe, David P., editor. Human Rights and Development: International Views. New York: St. Martin's Press; 1989. xvi, 369 p.

Franck, Thomas M. Human Rights in Third World Perspective. London, Rome, New York: Oceana Publications, Inc.; 1982. 3 volumes; ISBN: 0-379-20725-7.

Franck, Thomas M. Nation against Nation: what happened to the U.N. dream and what the U.S. can do about it. New York: Oxford University Press; 1985. viii, 334 p.; ISBN: 0-19-503587-9.

Freidlander, Robert A. Terrorism: Documents of International and Local Control. Dobbs Ferry, New York: Oceana Publications, Inc.; 1990. 576 p.; ISBN: 0-379-00690-1.

Garcia-Amador, F.V. The Emerging International Law of Development: A New Dimension of International Economic Law. New York; London; Rome: Oceana Publications; 1990. viii, 286p.; ISBN: 0-379-20221-2.

Galtung, Johan. The True Worlds: a transnational perspective. New York: Free Press; 1980. xxv, 469 p. (Preferred Worlds for the 1990's: World Order Models Project).

Galtung, Johan. There are Alternatives: Four Roads to Peace and Security. Nottingham, England; Chester Springs, Pennsylvania: Spokeman, Bertrand Russell House; Dufour Editions, Inc.; 1984. 221 p.; ISBN: 0-85124-393-2; 0-85124-394-0.

Giradot, Rafael Gutierrez, et al., editors. New Directions in International Law: essays in honour of Wolfgang Abendroth,Festschrift zu seinem 75. Geburtstag. Frankfurt/Main,ISBN: 3-593-33022-9. = Note: Preface in English and German; text in English, French or German./it =

Gorbachev, Mikhail Sergeevich. A Time for Peace. New York: Richardson and Stierman; 1984. 297 p.; ISBN: 0-931922-08-0.

Gorbachev, Mikhail Sergeevich. Perestroika. New Thinking for Our Country and the World. New York: Harper and Row; 1987. 254 p. (A Cornelia and Michael Bessie book.); ISBN: 0-06-0390859.

Gorove, Stephen. United States Space Law: National and International Regulation. Dobbs Ferry, New York: Oceana Publications; 1982--with current supplements. 3 binders. (International Law Looseleaf Services); ISBN: 0-379-20695- 1.

Gross, Leo. Essays on International Law and Organization. Dobbs Ferry, New York: Transnational Publishers; 1984. 2 vol.; ISBN: 0-941320-15-4.

Gross, Leo, editor. The Future of the International Court of Justice. Dobbs Ferry, New York: Oceana Press [for the American Society of International Law]; 1976. 2 vol. Note: Preface by Paul C. Jessup and Edvard Hambro.

Grzybowski, Kazimierz. Soviet International Law and the World Economic Order. Durham, North Carolina: Duke University Press; 1987. xii, 226 p. (Duke Press Policy Series); ISBN:0-8223- 0734-1. Note: update of Soviet Public International Law and Diplomatic Practice.

Gustafson, Lowell S. The Sovereignty Dispute over the Falkland (Malvinas) Islands. New York and Oxford: Oxford University Press; 1988. xiii, 268 p.

BIBLIOGRAPHY

Halderman, John W. The United Nations and the Rule of Law; Charter Development through the Handling of International Disputes and Situations. Dobbs Ferry, New York: Oceana Publications; 1966. 248 p.

Hannikainen, Lauri. Peremptory Norms (jus cogens) in International Law: Historical Development, Criteria, Present Status. Helsinki, Finland: Lakimiesliiton Kustannus, Finnish Lawyer's Publishing Company: 1988. xxxii, 781 p.

Hannum, Hurst. Autonomy, Sovereignty, and Self- Determination: The Accommodation of Conflicting Rights. Philadelphia: University of Pennsylvania Press: 1990. x, 503 p.

Hazard, John N. Recollections of a Pioneering Sovietologist. 2nd revised edition ed. London; Rome; and New York: Oceana Publications, Inc.; 1987. xxi, 188 p.

Henkin, Louis and Rosenthal, Albert J., editors. Constitutionalism and Rights: the Influence of the United States Constitution Abroad. New York: Columbia University Press; 1990. viii, 462 p.

Henkin, Louis; Hoffman, Stanley; Kirkpatrick, Jeane J.; Gerson, Allan; Rogers, William D.; Scheffer, David J. and foreword by John Temple Swing. Right V. Might: International Law and the Use of Force. New York and London: Council on Foreign Relations Press; 1989; ISBN: 0-87609-067-6.

Henkin, Louis. The Age of Rights. New York: Columbia University Press; 1990. xi, 220 p.

Hingorani, R.C. Studies in International Law. Dobbs Ferry, New York: Oceana Press; 1981. 115 p.

Hingorani, R.C. Modern International Law. 2nd ed. Dobbs Ferry, New York: Oceana Press; 1984. xii, 472 p.; ISBN: 0-379- 20447-9.

Hollins, Harry B.; Powers, Averill L.; and Sommer, Mark; with contributions by Kenneth Boulding and Roger Fisher (Alternative Defense Project). The Conquest of War: Alternative Strategies for Global Security. Boulder, San Francisco, and London: Westview Press; 1989. xii, 224 p.; ISBN: 0-8133-0786-4 (hdbk); 0-8133-0787- 2 (pbk).

Hoyt, Edwin C. Law and Force in American Foreign Policy. Lanham, Maryland: University Press of America; 1985. 270 p.; ISBN: 0-8191-4430-4.

Hufbauer, Gary Clyde, and Schott, Jefferey J. Economic Sanctions Reconsidered: History and Current Policy. Washington, D.C.: ISBN: 0-88132-017-X.

Irwin, Robert A. Building a Peace System. Washington, D.C.; New York: ExPro Press: Exploratory Project on the Conditions of Peace; Talman Company, distributor; 1989; ISBN: 0-936391-1 (pbk).

Jankowitsch, Odette, and Sauvant, K.P., editors. The Third World without Superpowers: the Collected Documents of Non- Aligned Countries. Dobbs Ferry, New York: Oceana Press; 1978. 4 v.;ISBN: 0-941320-19-7.

Jenks, C. Wilfred. The Prospects of International Adjudication. London; Dobbs Ferry, New York: Stevens and Sons Limited; Oceana Publications; 1964.

Joyce, James Avery. Human Rights: International Documents. Alphen aan den rijn, The Netherlands; Dobbs Ferry, New York:Sijthoff and Noordhoff; Oceana Publications, Inc.; 1978. 3 volumes; ISBN: 90-286-0298-4 (Sijthoff); 0-379-20395-2 (Oceana).

Joyner, Christopher C. and Chopra, Sudhir K., editors. The Antarctic Legal Regime. Dordrecht, Boston, and London: Martinus Nifhoff Publishers; 1988. x, 288 p.

Kennan, George F. The Nuclear Delusion: Soviet-American Relations in the Atomic Age. New York: Pantheon Books; 1982: 1700. xxx, 208 p.

BIBLIOGRAPHY

Kennedy, David. International Legal Structures. Baden- Baden, Germany: Nomos Verlagsgesellschaft; 1987. 294 p.; ISBN: 3- 7890-1367-6.

Kiang, John. One World: the Approach to Permanent Peace on Earth and the General Happiness of Mankind. A Popular Manifesto with Scholarly Annotations. Notre Dame: One World PublishingCompany; 1984. xv, 633 p.

Kim, Samuel S.. The Quest for a Just World Order. Boulder,Colorado: Westview Press; 1984. xix, 440 p. (Westview special studies in international relations); ISBN: 0- 86531-365-2.Note: Written under the auspices of the Center of International Studies, Princeton University.

Kincaide, William H., editor. The Access Resource Guide: An International Directory of Information on War, Peace and Security. Hayner, Priscilla B. Cambridge, Mass.: Ballinger Publishing Co.;1988; ISBN: 0-88730-260-2 / 0-88730-262-9 (pbk.).A guide to 657 institutions and organizations concerned with various peace issues.

Kleckner, Simone-Marie, compiler. Public International Law and International Organization. revised and updated ed. Dobbs Ferry, New York: Oceana Publications, Inc.; 1988. v, 126 p. (A Collection of Bibliographic and Research Resources); ISBN: 0-379- 20915-2 / 0-379-20890-3 (Series). An updating of the public international law and international organization section of Kleckner and Kudej's International Legal Bibliography (1983) which, in turn was based on "Public Selective Bibliography," U.N. Doc. ST/LIB/3 (1982).Approximately 1400 entries.

Kochler, Hans, editor. The International Information and Communication Order: Basis for Cultural Dialogue and Peaceful Coexistence among Nations. Vienna, Austria: W. Braumuller;1985. vi, 127 p. (Studies in International Relations / International Progress Organization, Vienna; no. 10); ISBN:3- 7003-0645-8. Note: Text in English or French.

Kohona, Palitha T.B. (Legal Division of the Department of Foreign Affairs of Australia). The Regulation of International Economic Relations through Law. Dordrecht; Boston; and Lancaster: Martinus Nijhoff Publishers; 1985. xxii, 280 p.;ISBN: 90-247-3104-6.

Kovalenko, Ivan Ivanovich and Tuzmukhamedov [or Touzmohammed], Rais A. The Non-Aligned Movement: the Soviet View. New Delhi, India: Sterling Publishers Private Ltd.; 1987. 176 p.

Krepon, Michael, editor. Verification and Compliance: A Problem-Solving Approach. Basingstoke: Macmillan; 1988. xvii, 308 p.; ISBN: 0-333-42606-8.

Kuper, Leo. The Prevention of Genocide. New Haven and London: Yale University Press; 1985. ix, 286 p.; ISBN: 0-300- 03418-0.

Lachs, Manfred. The Teacher in International Law: teachings and teaching. The Hague, Netherlands; Boston, Mass.: Martinus Nijhoff; 1982. 236 p.; ISBN: 90-247-2566-6.

Lambert, Joseph J. Terrorism and Hostages in International Law-A Commentary on the Hostages Convention 1979. Cambridge: Grotius Publications Limited; 1990. xxv, 418 p.

Lauterpacht, Hersch Sir. The Development of International Law by the International Court. revised ed.; (London: Stevens and Son's Ltd.; 1958), reprinted by: Cambridge: Grotius Publications Ltd.; 1982.

Lebedev, N.I. A New Stage in International Relations. Skvirsky, D. Ya. and Schneiderson, V.M., translators. Oxford; New York: Pergamon Press; 1978. xv, 253 p.

Levie, Howard S., editor. The Law of Non-International Armed Conflict: Protocol II to the 1949 Geneva Conventions. Dordrecht; Boston; and Lancaster: Martinus Nijhoff Publishers; 1987. xiii, 635 p.

Levie, Howard S. The Code of International Armed Conflict: Dobbs Ferry, New York: Oceana Publications; 2 vols. 1986

BIBLIOGRAPHY

Luard, Evan. Conflict and Peace in the Modern International System. 2nd completely revised edition ed. Basingstoke, England: Macmillan Press; 1988. xii, 318 p.; ISBN: 0- 333-44836-7.

Luard, Evan. The Blunted Sword: the erosion of military policy in modern world politics. London, England: I.B. Tauris and Co.;1988. 196 p.; ISBN: 1-85043-068-3.

Makarczyk, Jerzy, editor (Institute of State and Law in the Polish Academy of Sciences). Essays in International Law in Honour of Judge Manfred Lachs. The Hague, Netherlands; Boston, Mass.: M. Nijhoff; 1984. 757 p.; ISBN: 90-247-3071-6. Essays on the Theory of International Law, the International Court of Justice and Peaceful Settlement of Disputes, International Organizations, and the Law of the Sea and Outer Space.

Makarczyk, Jerzy. Principles of a New International Economic Order: A Study of International Law in the Making. Dordrecht,Boston, and London: Martinus Nijhoff Publishers; 1988. p. 367.

Malekian, Farhad. The System of International Law: Formation,Treaties, Responsibility. Uppsala; 1987. xii, 232 p.

Mandelbaum, Michael. The Fate of Nations: the Search for National Security in the Nineteenth and Twentieth Centuries.Cambridge, U.K.: Cambridge University Press; 1988. xi, 416p.; ISBN: 0-521-35527-3 - 0-521-35790-X.

Max Planck Institute for Comparative Public Law and International Law. Judicial Settlement of International Disputes:International Court of Justice, other courts and tribunals,arbitration and conciliation: an international symposium.West Berlin and New York: Springer-Verlag; 1974. xii, 572 p.(Beitrage zum Auslanddischen offentlichen Recht und Volkerrecht); ISBN: 3-540-06756-6 (Berlin); 0-387-06756-6(U.S.A.).

McDougal, Myres Smith et al. Studies in World Public Order. New Haven, Connecticut; Dordrecht, Netherlands: New Haven Press;Martinus Nijhoff Publishers; 1987. xxi, 1058 p. (The New Haven Studies in International Law and World Public Order);ISBN: 0-89838-900-3.

McDougal, Myres S.; Lasswell, Harold D.; and Chen, Lung- chu. Human Rights and World Public Order; the basic policies of an international law of human dignity. New Haven: Yale University Press; 1980. xxiv, 1016 p.

McDougal, Myres S. and Feliciano, Florentino P. Law and Minimum World Public Order. New Haven, Conn. and London, England: Yale University Press; 1967. xxvi, 872 p.

McKinlay, R. D. and Little, R. Global Problems and World Order. London: Frances Pinter, Publishers; 1986; ISBN: 0-903804- 46-8.

McWhinney, Edward. The International Law of Detente: Arms Control, European Security, and East-West Cooperation. Alphenaan den Rijn: Sijthoff and Noordhoff International Publishers; 1978: 1700. 259 p.

McWhinney, Edward. United Nations Law Making: cultural and ideological relativism and international law making for an era of transition. New York; Paris: Holmes and Meir; UNESCO:1984. xi, 274 p. (New challenges to international law making UNESCO; vol. 3); ISBN: 0-8419-0948-2 - 92-3-102147-8.

Meron, Theodor. Human Rights and Humanitarian Norms as Customary Law. Oxford, U.K.: Clarendon Press; 1989. x, 263 p.

Meyer, Michael A., editor. Armed Conflict and the New Law: Aspects of the 1977 Protocols and the 1981 Weapons Convention. British Institute of International and Comparative Law; London: 1989.

Mikus, Joseph A. Beyond Deterrence: from Power Politics to World Public Order. New York, Bern, Frankfurt am Main, Paris: Peter Lang; 1988. viii, 219 p. (American University Studies; Series X, Political Science; vol. 15); ISBN: 0-8204-0699-6.

Miller, Arthur Selwyn and Feinrider, Martin, editors. Nuclear Weapons and Law. Westport, Connecticut: Greenwood Press; 1984. xiii, 415 p. (Contributions in legal studies; no. 31); ISSN: 0147-1074; ISBN: 0-313-24206-2. Note: Several articles are based on remarks delivered at the Conference on Nuclear Weapons and Law held at the Nova Law Center on February 5, 1983.

Mische, Gerald and Mische, P. Toward a Human World Order; Beyond the National Security Straightjacket. New York: Paulist Press; 1977. 399 p.

Mitchell, C.R. and Webb, K., editors. New Approaches to International Mediation. New York; Westport, Connecticut; London: Greenwood Press; 1988.

Morgenthau, Hans J. Politics Among Nations: the Struggle for Power and Peace. 5th ed. New York: Alfred A Knopf; 1978. xxviii, 650 p.

Mosler, Hermann. The International Society as a Legal Community. revised ed. Alphen aan den Rijn, Netherlands; Germantown, Md.: Sijthoff and Noordhoff; 1980. xix, 327 p.Note: Originally published in Collected Courses / Hague Academy of International Law, v. 140 (1974-IV).

Murphy, John F. The United Nations and the Control of International Violence: a Legal and Political Analysis.Totowa, New Jersey: Allanheld, Osmun; 1982. xii, 212 p.;ISBN: 0-86598-079- 9.

Murphy, John F. Punishing International Terrorists: The Legal Framework for Policy Initiatives. Totowa, New Jersey: Rowman and Allanheld, Publishers; 1985. x, 142 p.

Murphy, John F. State Support of International Terrorism: Legal, Political, and Economic Dimensions. Boulder and San Francisco; London: Westview Press; Mansell Publishing Limited; 1989. vii, 128 p.

Murty, B.S. The International Law of Diplomacy: The Diplomatic Instrument and World Public Order. Dordrecht; Boston; London: Martinus Nijhoff Publishers; New Haven: New Haven Press; 1989.

Muskat, Marion. The Third World and Peace: some Aspects of the Interrelationship of Underdevelopment and International Security. Aldershot,

Hampshire, England; New York: Gower; St.Martin's Press; 1982: 1700. xviii, 260 p. (Israeli Institute for the Study of International Affairs). Note: includes bibliography.

Mutharika, A. Peter. Regulation of Statelessness under International and National Law: Texts and Documents. Dobbs Ferry, New York: Oceana Publications; 1977-1986. 2 binders.(International Law Looseleaf Services); ISBN: 0-379-10040-1.Acquisition and Loss of Nationality; Access by Stateless Persons to Foreign Territory.

Nelson, Ronald R. and Schweizer, Peter. The Soviet Concepts of Peace, Peaceful Coexistence and Detente,. Lanham: University Press of America; 1988. xvi, 177 p.; ISBN: 0-8191-6833- 5.

Nordquist, Myron H. and Park, Choon H. North America and Asia-Pacific and the Development of the Law of the Sea. Dobbs   Ferry, New York: Oceana Publications; 1980. 2 binders (International Law Looseleaf Services); ISBN: 0-379-20322-7. Note: Service now closed; updated by Simmonds' New Directions in the Law of the Sea.

Oellers-Frahm, Karin, and Wuhler, Norbert, compilers (Max Planck Institute for Comparative Public Law and International Law).Dispute Settlement in Public International Law: Texts and Materials. West Berlin and New York: Springer Verlag; 1984.xx, 913 p.; ISBN: 3-540-13190-6; 0-307-13190-6.

Osieke, Ebere. (University of Jos, Nigeria, and formerly a Member of the Legal Advisory Staff of the International Labor Office, Geneva, Switzerland). Constitutional Law and Practice   in the International Labour Organization. Dordrecht, Netherlands and Boston, Mass.: Martinus Nijhoff; 1985. xxi, 266 p. (Legal aspects of international organization; no. 5); ISBN: 90-247- 2985-8.

Ott, David H. Public International Law in the Modern World. London, England: Pitman; 1987. xxi, 390 p.; ISBN: 0-273- 02815-4.

Patchen, Martin. Resolving Disputes between Nations: Coercion or Conciliation. Durham, N.C.: Duke University Press; 1988. xiii, 365 p. (Duke Press Policy Studies); ISBN: 0-8223-0764- 2-0-8223-0819-3.

BIBLIOGRAPHY

Platzoder, Renate. The Law of the Sea: Documents 1983-1989: The Preparatory Commission for the International Sea-Bed Authority and for the International Tribunal for the Law of the Sea. Dobbs Ferry, New York: Oceana Publications, Inc.; 1990. 10 volumes; ISBN: 0-379-20973-7.

Pontecorvo, Guilio, editor. The New Order of the Oceans: the Advent of a Managed Environment. New York: Columbia University Press; 1986. xv, 277 p.

Ramcharan, B.G. The International Law Commission; its Approach to the Codification and Progressive Development of International Law. The Hague, Netherlands: Martinus Nijhoff; 1977. xvi, 227 p.

Ramcharan, B.G., editor (Special Assistant to the Director, UN Division of Human Rights). The Right to Life in International Law. Dordrecht, Netherlands and Boston, Mass.: 1985. xii, 371 p. (International Studies in Human Rights); ISBN: 90-247- 3074-0.

Ramcharan, B.G. editor. International Law and Fact-Finding in the Field of Human Rights. The Hague, Netherlands; Boston, Mass.: Martinus Nijhoff; 1982. x, 259 p. (International Studies in Human Rights); ISBN: 90-247-3042-2.

Ramcharan, B.G. The Concept and Present Status of the International Protection of Human Rights: Forty Years After the Universal Declaration. Dordrecht, Boston and London: Martinus Nijhoff Publishers; 1989. xi, 611 p.

Rawnsley, L. Scott and McWhirter, Jay D. Selective Bibliography of Outer Space Law. Dobbs Ferry, New York: Oceana Publications; 1987. (A Collection of Bibliographic and Research Resources). Note: Also available in the 2-binder 13-bibliography set, "A Collection of Bibliographic and Research Resources," ISBN: 0-379-20890-3.

Reardon, Betty A. Comprehensive Peace Education: Educating for Global Responsibility. New York and London: Teachers College Press, Columbia University; 1988; ISBN: 0-8077-2885-3.

Reisman, W. Michael and Willard, Andrew R., editors.International Incidents: The Law That Counts in World Politics. Princeton, New Jersey: Princeton University Press; 1988. xii, 278 p.

Renniger, John P., editor. The Future Role of the United Nations in an Interdependent World. Dordrecht, Boston and London: Martinus Nijhoff Publishers; 1989. xviii, 283 p.

Rodman, Kenneth A. Sanctity Versus Sovereignty: The United States and the Nationalization of Natural Resource Investments. New York: Columbia University Press; 1988. xvii, 403 p.

Rosenne, Shabtai. The World Court: What It Is and How It Works. 4th revised ed.: Dordrecht, Boston and London; Martinus Nijhoff Publishers; (1989). xv, 320 p.

Rosenne, Shabtai. Practice and Methods of International Law. London, England and Dobbs Ferry, New York: Oceana Publications; 1984. xi, 169 p.; ISBN: 0-379-20140-2.

Rotblat, Joseph, editor. Coexistence, Cooperation and Common Security: Annals of Pugwash. Basingstoke: Macmillan; 1988; ISBN: 0-333-46587-3.

Rudden, Bernard and Wyatt, Derrick, editors. Basic Community Laws. Oxford, England: Clarendon Press; 1986. xiv, 407 p.;ISBN: 0-19-876199-6.

Ruster, Bernd and Simma, Bruno. International Protection of the Enviornment. Dobbs Ferry, New York: Oceana Publications;1989. 31 volumes and a current looseleaf binder; ISBN:' 0-379-10086-X. Note: The complete set is the most comprehensive documentation of environmental law in the world.

Saxena, J.N.; Gurdip Singh; and Koul, A.K., editors. United Nations for a Better World. New Delhi, India: Lancers Books; 1986. xv, 313 p. Note: Foreword by Dr. Nagendra Singh, President of the International Court of Justice.

BIBLIOGRAPHY

Schwebel, Stephen M. International Arbitration: Three Salient Problems. Cambridge: Grotius Publications Limited; 1987. xviii, 303 p.

Schwebel, Stephen M., editor. The effectiveness of International Decisions: Papers of a Conference of the American Society of International Law, and the Proceedings of the Conference. Leyden; Dobbs Ferry, New York; A.W. Sijthoff; Oceana Publications, Inc.; 1971. 538 p.; ISBN: 90-218-9041-0.

Sebek, Victor. Eastern European States and the Development of the Law of the Sea: Regional Documents, National Legislation.Dobbs Ferry, New York: Oceana Publications; 1976-. 2 binders. (International Law Looseleaf Services); ISBN: 0-379-10185- 88.Note: Set now closed; updated by Butler's the USSR, Eastern Europe and the Development of the Law of the Sea.

Sherr, Avrom. Freedom of Protest, Public Order and the Law.Oxford, England and New York, New York: Basil Blackwell; 1989. xvii, 223 p.; ISBN: 0-631-15809-X (hdbk); 0-631-15811-1 (pbk)

Sieghart, Paul. The Lawful Rights of Mankind: an Introduction to the International Legal Code of Human Rights. Oxford, England and New York: Oxford University Press; 1985. xviii, 252 p.; ISBN: 0-19-219190-X.

Simmonds, Kenneth R. New Directions in the Law of the Sea. Dobbs Ferry, New York: Oceana Publications; 1983--with current supplements. 5 binders (International Law Looseleaf Services); ISBN: 0-379-16550.

Singh, Nagendra, and Mcwhinney, Edward. Nuclear Weapons and Contemporary International Law. 2nd revised edition. ed.Dordrecht, Boston, and London: Martinus Nijhoff Publishers;1989. xxvi, 611 p. (Developments in International Law; vol.11); ISBN: 90-247-3637-4.

Sinha, Surya Prakash. Asylum and International Law. The Hague, Netherlands: Martinus Nijhoff; 1971. xii, 366 p.

Sinha, Surya Prakash. New Nations and the Law of Nations. Leyden: A.W. Sitjhoff; 1967. 176 p.

Sivard, Ruth Leger. World Military and Social Expenditures.(13th edition appeared in 1989) ed. Washington D.C.: World Priorities; Normally annual, occasionally every other year.

Snyder, Frederick E. and Sathirathai, Surakiart, editors. Third World Attitudes toward International Law: an Introduction. Dordrecht, Netherlands and Boston, Mass.: Martinus Nijhoff Publishers; 1987. xx, 850 p.; ISBN: 0-89838-914-3.

Sohn, Louis B., editor. International Organization and Integration: Annotated Basic Documents and Descriptive Directory of International Organizations and Arrangements. 2nd revised ed. Hingham Mass.: Martinus Nijhoff; 1981-1984.5 vols.: IA: 1322 p.; IB: 760 p.; IIA: 640 p.; IIB: 970 p.;IIK: 852 p.; ISBN: Vol.IA: 90-247-2579-8; IB: 90-247-2657-3;IIA: 90-247-2587-9; IIB: 90-247-2587- 9; IIK: 90-247-2952-1.VOL. IA: The United Nations Organization; IB: Organizations Related to the United Nations; IIA: European Communities; IIB: Other Organizations and Arrangements; IIK: Functional Organizations and Arrangements.

Spinedi, Marina and Simma, Marina, editors. United Nations Codification of State Responsibility. New York, London, and Rome: Oceana Publications, Inc.; 1987. xi, 418 p.

Stone, Julius. Visions of World Order: between State Power and Human Justice. Baltimore, Maryland: Johns Hopkins University Press; 1984. xxix, 246 p.; ISBN: 0-8018-3174-1.

Sud, Usha. Decolonization to World Order: international organizations and the emerging pattern of global interdependence. New Delhi, India: National Publishing House; 1983. xiv, 347 p.; ISBN: 139-9-11-1282.

Suter, Keith D. Alternative to War: Conflict Resolution and the Peaceful Settlement of International Disputes. 2nd ed.Sydney, Australia: Women's International League for Peace and Freedom; 1986. vi, 151 p.; ISBN: 0-909506-15-9.

BIBLIOGRAPHY

Suter, Keith D. Peaceworking: the United Nations and Disarmament. Sydney, New South Wales, Australia: United Nations Association of Australia; 1985: 1440. 189 p.; ISBN: 0- 949652-407.

Suter, Keith D. The International Law of Guerrilla Warfare: the global politics of law-making. New York, New York: St.Martin's Press; 1984. x, 192 p. (Global Politics Series); ISBN: 0-312- 42290-3. Note: Based on a doctoral dissertation written at the University of Sydney.

Suter, Keith D. Reshaping the Global Agenda: the U.N. at 40. Sydney, Australia: United Nations Association of Australia; 1986. 119 p.; ISBN: 0-949652-01-6.

Szasz, Paul C. The Law and Practices of the International Atomic Energy Agency. Vienna: International Atomic Energy Agency; 1970. 1176 p. (IAEA Legal Series; no. 7).

Szekely, Alberto. Latin America and the Development of the Law of the Sea: Regional Documents; National Legislation. Dobbs Ferry, New York: Oceana Publications; 1976. 2 binders.(International Law Looseleaf Services); ISBN: 0-379-10180- 7.

Tajima, Mikio, editor. Peace through Economic Justice: essays in memory of Manuel Perez-Guerro. Geneva, Switzerland: Imprimerie Genevoise; 1988. v, 131 p.

Tardu, Maxine. Human Rights: the International Petition System. Dobbs Ferry, New York: Oceana Publications; 1979-1986. 3 binders; ISBN: 0-379-20250-6.

Taubenfeld, Howard S. and Taubenfeld, Rita F., compilers. Sex-Based Discrimination: International Law and Organization. Dobbs Ferry, New York: Oceana Publications; 1978-1983. 4 binders. (International Law Looseleaf Services); ISBN: 0-379-10139-4.

A collection of all treaties and other international acts concerning women; resolutions and case studies from international organizations; the rights of women under the OAS, the E.C.. Islamic law, and in Africa and Asia, the International

Decade of Women; and constitutional provisions from countries around the world and selected comparative laws.

Tolley, Howard Jr. The U.N. Commission on Human Rights. Boulder, Colorado, U.S.A. and London, U.K.: Westview Press; 1987. xv, 300 p.

Tomansevski, Katarina, editor. The Right to Food: a guide through applicable international law. Dordrecht, Netherlands; Boston, Mass.; and Lancaster Pa.: Martinus Nijhoff Publishers; 1987. xix, 387 p.; ISBN: 90-247-3365-0.

Tunkin, Grigorii I. Law and Force in the International System. Aksyonov, Yevgeny, translator from Russian. Moscow: Progress Publishers; 1985. 338 p.

Tutorow, Norman E. with assistance of Winnovich, Karen, compiler and editor. War Crimes, War Criminals, and War Crime Trials: an annotated bibliography and source book. London, England; New York, New York; and Westport, Connecticut: Greenwood Press; 1986. (Bibliographies and indexes in world history; no. 4); ISSN: 0742-06852; ISBN: 0-313-24412-X.

Umbricht, Victor H. Multilateral Mediation: Practical Experiences and Lessons. Cht; Boston; London: Martinus Nijhoff Publishers; 1988. ISBN: 90-247-3779-6.

United Nations Association in the USSR. The United Nations Organization Today: 40th anniversary of the UN. Moscow: Novosti Press Agency Pub. house; 1985. 109 p. Note: Translated from Russian.

United Nations Department of Public Information. The Blue Helmets: A Review of United Nations Peace-keeping. New York:United Nations; 1985; (ST/DPI/850; UN Sales No.; E.85.I.18):1440. vi, 350 p.

Vayrynen, Raimo; Senghaas, Dieter; and Schmidt, Christian, editors. The Quest for Peace: Transcending Collective Violence and War among Societies, Cultures and States. Javier Perez de Cuellar, author of foreword. London, England and Beverly Hills, California: Sage Publications; 1987. xii, 356 p.; ISBN: 0-8039-8035-3 - 0-8034-5. Note: Published in association with the International Social Sciences Council.

BIBLIOGRAPHY

Weiss, Edith Brown. In Fairness to Future Generations:International Law, Common Patrimony, and Intergenerational Equity. Tokyo, Japan; Dobbs Ferry, New York, U.S.A.: The United Nations University; Transnational Publishers, Inc.;1989. xixx, 385 p.

Weston, Burns H. Alternative Security, Living Without Nuclear weapons. Boulder, Co; Westview, 1990, 283 p. ISBN:0-8133-0629-9.

Weston, Burns H; Falk, Richard A.; and D'Amato, Anthony A. Basic Documents in International Law and World Order. St. Paul, Minnesota: West Pub. Co.; 1980. xiii, 447 p.

Willets, Peter, editor. Pressure Groups in the Global System: the transnational relations of issue-oriented non- governmental organizations. New York, New York: St. Martin's Press; 1982. xv, 225 p. (Global Politics Series.); ISBN: 0-312-64162-1.

Winham, Gilbert R., editor. New Issues in International Crisis Management. Boulder, Colorado Westview Press; 1988. x, 258 p. (New approaches to peace and security); ISBN: 0-8133-7295-X.

Woito, Robert S. To End War: A New Approach to International Conflict. 6th ed. Pickus, Robert. New York: Pilgrim Press; 1982. xx, 755 p.; ISBN: 0-8298-0464-1 / 0-8298-0476-5 (pbk.).

World Commission on Enviornment and Development. Our Common Future [The Brundtland Report]. Oxford; New York: Oxford University Press; 1987. xv, 400 p.; ISBN: 0-19-282080-X (pbk.).

Zarjevski, Yefime. A Future Preserved: International Assistance to refugees. Oxford and New York: Pergamon Press; 1988. xiv, 280 p.

Zhivkov, Todor. Peace and Security for the Peoples: the Helsinki Conference on Security and Cooperation in Europe: Ten Years After. Sofia: Sofia Press; 1985: 1440. 276 p.

Zhukov, Gennadii Petrovich, and Kolosov, Yuri. International Space Law. Boris Belitsky, trans. New York: Praeger; 1984. xiv, 224 p. (Praeger Special Studies; Praeger Scientific; published in cooperation with the Novisti Press Agency, Moscow); ISBN: 0-03-069812-X.